D1604115

the beast of
REVELATION 13

by
BOB FRALEY

Other Books by Bob Fraley

THE LAST DAYS IN AMERICA

HOLY FEAR

the beast of
REVELATION
13

by
BOB FRALEY

ISBN — 0-9612999-2-4

Published by
Christian Life Services
6438 East Jenan Drive
Scottsdale, Arizona 85254

Printed in the United States of America

DEDICATION

To help the Body of Christ
prepare for the spiritual challenges
in these troubled times.

CONTENTS

List of Illustrations

PREFACE

It was the fall of 1969 when the Lord guided my wife Barbara and me to take six children whose parents had been killed in a tragic automobile accident. Twenty-five years later, these six children, along with our own three, our sons and daughters-in-law and sixteen grandchildren total 35. Except for some of the grandchildren who are too young, they are all dedicated servants of the Lord.

Raising children in these troubled times is a challenge. Barbara and I have shared the spiritual principles we have followed by teaching Bible classes throughout the years, and I have written about the biblical foundation of living the Christian life in America during these times in two books, **The Last Days in America** and **Holy Fear.** But more than anything else, it has been our knowledge of a prophetic truth that has helped us raise our children according to biblical standards and avoid many of the spiritual pitfalls in these last days. *This truth, which I found the Scriptures confirm, is that the United States Government has become the beast-superpower of Revelation 13.* The Apostle John warns of how God's enemy, Satan, will use this end-time superpower to attack the standards and commitment of God's people.

After Barbara and I assumed the responsibility of raising these six children, and the Lord led me to study the Scriptures concerning this prophetic concept, we began to see the beast's system behind the frightful deterioration in the moral fabric of our society. We realized that if we did not take a godly stand to protect our family from many of the anti-Christian influences developing in our society, we could be overwhelmed by the moral holocaust unfolding across America. We were privileged to know about the beast's identity over 20 years ago; now the moral poverty of our nation is painfully obvious.

In two previous books, and numerous classes I have taught over the years, I review the biblical and historical evidence surrounding the conclusion that the United States Government has become the beast-superpower of Revelation 13—a startling prophetic concept. There have been many requests for a Bible study guide of these truths that could be shared with others. In this book, I provide a comprehensive Bible study guide to what I have discovered from my investigation.

For those who believe that John refers to a man in these verses from Revelation, Chapter 13, what I say about the United States Government may be hard to accept. The image of a man who rises from obscurity to world prominence shapes so much of the contemporary interpretation of end-time events. It is an idea that has become a major teaching of the doctrine of last things. I have found that the Greek translation of Scripture reveals that idea to be wrong. By close examination of those portions of Revelation and Daniel that refer to the beast, it is possible to understand the place of the United States Government in end-times prophecy. I then briefly explain what I believe this truth means, and make a few comments about how the beast affects everyday life. (How the beast affects everyday life is covered in much greater detail in my other two books.)

My purpose here is not to criticize those who offer a different interpretation. I want you to know that is not my heart. To criticize other believers would hardly be worth the expense to myself, or my time in writing and distributing this book. My heart's desire is to explain what I have learned about these prophetic passages and to encourage you to investigate them for yourself.

No one can be harmed by such investigation, because whether the investigation leads to truth or falsehood, the investigator reaps a reward for undertaking the search. If the investigation leads to truth, the investigator would have missed it had the effort not been made to find it. If the investigation leads to falsehood, the investigator has been strengthened from the experience of detecting error. A Christian who knows what he or she believes, and why, possesses a more sound and sure faith. That person will not suffer from investigating a potential new truth.

That is not to say truth needs no protection. Truth must be guarded against ignorance, willful error, and dishonesty. Scripture teaches that there will be those during the end time who will lead believers astray. False prophets that spin webs of deception will arise to trap the naive and unaware. This is why I challenge you to read further. Do not accept my word for it. Prayerfully consider what is written on the pages that follow. One thing I will assure you of: the content will draw you closer, not take you away, from your commitment to Jesus. I firmly believe that your investigation will help you gain the spiritual wisdom needed for your Christian walk in these last days.

Bob Fraley

INTRODUCTION

The word "beast" in the English language invokes the image of an animal, a wild and ferocious creature. A person who behaves "beastly" displays an animalistic lack of self-control. The beast of Bible prophecy is also associated with the "anti-Christ," the image of which is the very personification of evil. According to much contemporary Christian thinking, the anti-Christ, the opposite of Jesus Christ, fills the world with wickedness in a challenge to God near the end of time.

Regrettably, these English words, and the images they invoke, reinforce a particular notion of the beast of Bible prophecy. That is, the idea that the beast of Revelation 13 refers to a man who, appearing on the world stage, exercises great power. In this popular interpretation, the beast is a dictator who exercises worldwide dominance. This man, who acts in a brutal, coarse, vile manner to further his evil ends, assumes such power after returning from death.

The image of a one-man-world-dictator interferes with our ability to grasp the true beast of Bible prophecy. As it is used in prophetic scripture, the word "beast" symbolizes a governmental power. John uses the word "beast" simply to describe a dominant world government. He refers to wild animals, such as a lion and a bear, to represent mighty, powerful empires. In the book of Daniel, wild animals are used to represent the same thing: a worldwide empire, or what we might call today, a *superpower*.

It is important to realize that when Jesus was born in Bethlehem, he was born under a government called a beast in Scripture. When the apostles built the church upon the foundation laid by Jesus, they too lived under a beast-superpower. Rome is called a beast because of its position then as a world power. John uses some of the same prophetic phrases to describe the beast-superpower in Revelation 13 that are used elsewhere to refer to the Roman government.

1

The truth of what I am saying is verifiable by the Scriptures. Before beginning a verse-by-verse examination of those passages of Revelation 13 that refer to the beast, I want to make clear my approach to the interpretation of prophetic Scripture. My own study has been guided by three principles:

(1) There is no higher authority for interpreting the inspired Word of God than the source of that inspiration. God reveals His truth through revelation and through Scripture. No author of a Bible book writing about the same topic will contradict another. The Scriptures never fail to be consistent. So if an interpretation holds for one passage, it will hold for another passage.

(2) In order to understand passages and words it is often necessary to study the original languages. The Old Testament was written in Hebrew, the New Testament in Greek. Understanding prophetic words and phrases often requires learning the original Greek or Hebrew word or phrase, and what that word or phrase meant to the Hebrew or Greek author who wrote it. Idioms cannot be deciphered without learning what the word or idea meant in the context of Jewish life and culture at that time.

(3) Historical evidence either confirms that a prophecy has already been fulfilled, or that it is yet to be fulfilled. Prophesies are statements about future events, either they happen as foretold or they don't. If a prophecy can be said to have been fulfilled in reference to a particular place and time, then the evidence uncovered by archaeologists and historians about that place and time will be consistent with that prophecy.

These three principles are listed in order of priority. The first, and then the second principles must be followed by the third. To apply prophetic passages to historical events without reference to other prophetic passages will lead to mistaken interpretation. Using history alone also invites speculation because historical knowledge is inexact. If the present state of information about a historical event increases, a historically-based prophecy may falter. Moving the interpretation of Bible prophecy outside the realm of speculation and conjecture then, demands a thorough reading and comparison of the Scripture.

The Revelation to John

In the book of Revelation, John prophetically describes the last-days superpower he refers to as the "beast." These passages from Revelation, together with several verses in the book of Daniel, provide the insight from the Word of God necessary for us to learn the identity of the beast.

Many church historians believe that the same John wrote both Revelation and the Gospel of John. John, the son of Zebedee, was one of the twelve disciples. Originally a convert of John the Baptist, the son of Zebedee transferred his loyalty to Christ at John the Baptist's suggestion. John, who refers to himself as the "beloved disciple," leaned his head on Jesus' chest during the last supper, and at Peter's request, asked Jesus to tell who would betray him. As one of the chosen twelve, John was present at many of the occasions recorded in his Gospel, including the wedding at Cana, the feeding of the five thousand, and the raising of Lazarus.

Most likely, John wrote Revelation in exile. According to church history, he spent his last years at Ephesus before his banishment to the Isle of Patmos by the Roman emperor Domitian in about 95 AD. The revelation to John, the last book of the Bible, begins with messages to the seven churches in Asia, then in chapter 4, provides a description of a heavenly scene followed by the opening of the seven-sealed book, the sounding of seven trumpets, and description of the earthly events they announce. Then, in Revelation 12, the scene changes. It is in this chapter that John gives us an overview of some of the major events in God's plan for the salvation of mankind before he introduces the end-time beast-superpower in Revelation 13. It is here he begins his discussion of the symbols used in connection with the beast, and in order to properly understand Chapter 13, it is necessary to review several of the symbols that appear in Chapter 12.

A Woman Clothed with the Sun

The twelfth chapter opens with the appearance of a great wonder in the sky, *"a woman clothed with the sun."* The woman, who symbolizes God's family here on earth, wears luminous clothing—the sun and the moon, or that element of God's creation that controls the functioning of natural elements on the earth. She also wears a *"crown of twelve stars on her head,"* indicating that she represents a people with twelve parts or entities. These stars represent the twelve tribes of Israel, and the woman, the Jewish nation and its people.

Understanding God's relationship with the Jewish nation opens the door to end-time events. The history of the Jewish people consumes the greatest portion of the Bible itself, the Old Testament. The first eleven chapters of Genesis provide a history of the world in general, then in chapter 12, the biblical account shifts to the biography of a single man, Abraham, and to the everlasting covenant God made with him. God promised to make Abraham's descendants into a great nation (Genesis 12:1-3).

The remainder of Genesis tells of Abraham's son Isaac, and his son Jacob, whose twelve sons began the twelve tribes of Hebrews. It tells of Joseph, and of the Hebrews' captivity in Egypt. The great exodus, led by Moses, follows, as does the Hebrews' settlement in the land of Canaan (or Palestine, as it is to be called later, after the native Philistines). The first kingdom was established under David, and during the reign of his son Solomon, the Jewish people reached their golden age as a civilization. After Solomon, God's people split into two separate kingdoms—Israel, comprising the ten original tribes, and Judah, comprising the remaining two. Israel has come to refer to the Jewish nation; the word "Jew" is simply an abbreviation of "Judean."

In the second verse of Revelation chapter 12, John describes how the sun-clad woman *"cried out in her pangs of birth, in anguish for delivery"* (RSV). Here, John speaks of the purpose God had intended for His people from the beginning. From the time He formed Israel as a nation, God intended for His people to perform one mission—to give birth to the Son of God (Galatians 3:16-29).

The remainder of the Old Testament chronicles these birth pangs. Beginning with Isaiah, God sent the sixteen writing prophets to reclaim His people from their idolatry. But God's people persisted in their sin, and God disciplined them. The northern kingdom received judgment first, falling captive to the Assyrians in 722 BC. The two southern tribes were taken captive by the Babylonians, who sacked Jerusalem in 586 BC. When the Babylonians later conquered the Assyrians, all twelve tribes were together again. Then seventy years later, the Babylonians fell to the Persians.

The Persian King Cyrus allowed the Israelites to return to Palestine as prophesied by Isaiah three hundred years earlier (Isaiah 45:13). The Jewish people occupied the land given to their forefathers Abraham, Isaac, and Jacob, but they were not free of foreign domination. Politically, they were controlled for the next six hundred years by a succession of foreign powers; first the Persians, then the Greeks and Syrians, and finally, the Romans.

A Great Red Dragon

In Revelation 12:3, another major symbol appears just as the woman is about to fulfill her mission and give birth, that of *"an enormous red dragon."* The dragon, or Satan, waits for the woman, Israel, to give birth, in order that *"he might devour her child the moment it was born"* (Revelation 12:4). Here John reveals Satan's attempt to thwart God's plan for the redemption of mankind by having Israel's son, Jesus, killed.

In verses 5 through 12, John recounts the protection afforded to the woman who gave birth to the male child, and of a war in heaven, in which the angels of God cast Satan down to earth. I believe this battle took place at the death of Jesus, when the Saviour's blood was given to conquer Satan. While I do not understand many of the activities in the spiritual realm, it appears that until Jesus ascended to the right hand of God the Father, Satan had access to the throne of God where he continuously accused the children of God (Job 1,2). What is clear, however, is that Satan had never before suffered a defeat quite like the one John describes in these verses, because Satan had been previously cast out of the heavens (Isaiah 14:12, Luke 10:18). What is important in these verses to understanding the beast, has to do with Satan's pursuit of Israel after being *"cast down to earth,"* and of God's plan for her protection.

John says that Satan pursued Israel after landing on the earth, but that Israel was given *"the two wings of a great eagle"* so that she could fly to a place of nourishment for *"a time, times and half a time"* (verse 14). The dragon's horns, heads, and crowns (verse 3) indicate the mechanism Satan used to pursue the birth of Christ, and the phrase *"time, times and half a time"* indicates God's plan for Israel's preservation. John uses some of this same prophetic language in chapter 13, and I will discuss it in greater detail in my analysis of those verses.

In short, horns, heads, and crowns are symbols of an earthly authority, which both scriptural and historical evidence point to as the Roman Empire. Satan used this powerful world empire to attack Christ while he lived on the earth. When the New Testament opens with Jesus' birth in Bethlehem, the Jewish people were living in Palestine under Roman rule, specifically, under the reign of King Herod.

The Roman Empire, the greatest power in world history to date, dominated the ancient world for 500 years. At the zenith of its rule, Roman influence extended east to the Caspian Sea, north to the forests of Britain and Germany, west to the Atlantic coast of Spain, and south along the Mediterranean coast of Africa. Satan used the might of Rome along with King Herod in his attempt to destroy Christ when Herod murdered all the male children two years and younger just after Jesus' birth.

In 70 AD, the Roman army destroyed Jerusalem, and began, I believe, the *"time, times and half a time"* John speaks of in verse 14. Jewish scribes used this phrase to refer to an unknown period of troublesome time that lingers—and lingers —and lingers. Specifically, I believe we now can see it refers to the Diaspora, the 1900-year period of dispersal of Jews throughout the world. Many Jews fled to Italy and Spain, many more as far away as China and Ethiopia. Scattered elements settled in Europe until the eleventh century, when Spain became the center of Jewish life under Moslem rule. Then in 1492, with the expulsion of Jewish people from Spain after a century of persecution by the Catholic Church, Jews concentrated in Eastern Europe. In Germany, Russia, and Poland, Jews lived in enclaves until the Nazi massacres of the 1930s and 1940s, when as many as two-fifths of the Jewish people lost their lives.

Persecution provoked many Jews to return to their homeland during the nineteenth and twentieth centuries, culminating with the creation of the State of Israel in 1948. On May 14 of that year, when the United Nations recognized the new nation, it was the first time the Jewish people controlled the land given to Abraham since the Babylonian King Nebuchadnezzar besieged it in 606 BC.

Through two millennia of dispersion and persecution, God fulfilled His promise to Abraham and preserved His descendants, culminating in a second restoration when the Jewish people returned to Palestine as prophesied by Isaiah (Isaiah 11:11-12), by Jeremiah (Jeremiah 16:14-15), and by Ezekiel (Ezekiel 11:16-17).

The Rest of Her Offspring

In Revelation 12:17, John shifts the focus of his prophetic words to Abraham's second family. He writes that the dragon, angered by the protection afforded Israel, *"went off to make war against the rest of her offspring."* It is *"the rest of her offspring,"* not the Jewish people, that are the reference point for Revelation chapter 13.

These people are those brought about through the male child the woman bore who was Jesus Christ. Abraham's first family, Israel, includes all of Abraham's descendants by physical birth; the second family are all Abraham's descendants by spiritual rebirth. All those people who accept Christ as their personal Saviour comprise Abraham's second family (see Romans 4:11-17; Galatians 3:8-29). They are the Christians, the Body of Christ, the church, or as John puts it here in Revelation 12:17, *"those who obey God's commandments and hold to the testimony of Jesus."*

Christ's birth, death, and resurrection allowed Gentiles to enter the Kingdom of God. The New Testament records the beginning of the church upon the foundation laid by Jesus Christ, and the early history of the church after Pentecost, when God poured out his Holy Spirit (Acts 2:1-4; John 14:15-17).

For nearly two thousand years, Satan has attacked the church through relentless persecution and deception. The Roman Empire represents the first instrument of this persecution. Between 64 AD and 306 AD, more than three million Christians were hunted down and tortured to death by 23 Roman emperors. Satan continued his pursuit of the "rest" of the woman's offspring, who had settled in Europe, using other earthly authorities. During the Dark Ages, the period of time from the fall of Rome to the Reformation, millions of early Christians were tortured for their faith. They faced the inquisitions, crusades, and reformation wars, which claimed millions of lives. Just as God allowed persecution of the Jewish people to move them to return to Palestine, He used persecution to move the center of Christianity out of Europe, to a new land across the sea.

The first sentence of Chapter 13, reads, *"And the dragon stood on the shore of the sea."* This reference to an ocean beach speaks to the movement of those who testify of Jesus from the Old World to the New World. Historically, this occurred after the reformation, when thousands of Christians, the Puritans, crossed from Europe to North America. In the New World, the Great Awakening led to the American Revolution and the founding of a new nation, whose government was grounded on Christian principles. As this new nation became the geographic center of Christianity during the modern era, Satan made it the battleground of his relentless pursuit of the woman and her offspring. It is Abraham's second family, preserved in the United States, that is the reference point for the events John prophesies about in Revelation 13, specifically, the beast, which appears in Revelation 13:1.

CHAPTER ONE

REVELATION 13:1

*And I saw a beast coming out of the sea. He had
ten horns and seven heads, with ten crowns on his
horns, and on each head a blasphemous name.*

Horns, heads, and crowns. At first glance, John's symbolic
language seems difficult to decipher. But a careful reading of this
verse reveals six points, corresponding to six key descriptive words
and phrases: (1) "beast," (2) "coming out of the sea," (3) "ten horns,"
(4) "seven heads," (5) "ten crowns on his horns," and (6) "blasphemous name on each head."

The Beast

The first word is most important. Before anything else will
make sense, the meaning of this word must be absolutely clear.
To confirm its meaning, it is necessary to examine the book of
Daniel in which a similar beast appears. It is not possible to
resort to a higher authority to understand God's Word than to
refer to other Scripture, as Jesus himself would often do. The
prophet Daniel speaks of a ten-horned beast in Chapter 7, and
learns its meaning from an angel.

During the reign of the Babylonian King Belshazzar, Daniel
awoke, troubled by a vision. While lying on his bed, he saw four
beasts driven by the wind out of the sea. To three of these beasts

he gives the names of known animals—a lion, a bear, a leopard—but the fourth he simply refers to as a ten-horned beast with iron teeth and bronze claws. Daniel asked an angel to explain what the vision meant, and the angel told him. *"The four great beasts,"* the angel said, *"are four kingdoms that will rise from the earth"* (Daniel 7:17). When Daniel asked about the fourth beast that differed from the others, the angel said: *"The fourth beast is a fourth kingdom that will appear on earth"* (Daniel 7:23).

This passage from Daniel shows that when the word "beast" appears in prophetic Scripture it refers to a powerful governmental authority—a kingdom, an empire, or a superpower. Daniel used the word "beast" in writing about the vision he had, and John uses the word in the same way.

But a current interpretation of Revelation 13:1 is that the beast refers to a man. This idea runs contrary to the angel's interpretation of Daniel's beasts, and stems from an incorrect rendering of the Greek word for beast used in this verse.

The pronouns used in Revelation, which refer to the beast, appear to support the idea that the beast of Revelation refers to a man. The King James and the New International Version, for example, translate the pronouns with "he," "his," and "him." But other Bible translations, such as the Revised Standard Version and Phillips Translation, use the word "it" which is consistent with the idea that the "beast" refers to a government entity. To find the correct translation requires a closer look at grammar.

In English, a pronoun must be of the same gender as its antecedent, the noun it replaces. Therefore, the English pronoun selected to refer to the English noun "beast" would depend on the gender of the Greek word for beast. If the Greek word for beast is masculine, then "he," "his," and "him," are the appropriate pronouns. But if the Greek word for beast is neuter, then "it" and "its" are proper.

The Greek word for beast in this verse is *therion*—neuter gender. The proper English rendering of John's writing then should be the neuter pronoun "it," which means John, like Daniel, is describing a governmental superpower with the word "beast." This is not a hypothetical answer but a grammatical fact.

This means, of course, that the King James and NIV translators supplied the wrong pronoun. Publishers of these translations agree with this point. This incorrect translation here is very misleading because it encourages the thought that "beast" refers to a man. Publishers of the Bible agree, the masculine pronoun is not grammatically correct. But because the traditional teaching is that the beast is a man, they have chosen to offer the wrong pronouns.[1]

Out of the Sea

This phrase also appears in Daniel, and so the angel's interpretation of Daniel's vision can also be used to understand John's vision. Daniel writes, *"Four great beasts, each different from the others, came up out of the sea"* (Daniel 7:3).

Daniel's four beasts (Daniel 7:1-7) refer to the succession of great world powers which shaped Israel's history before the time of Christ. The lion represents Babylon, a nation which conquered Egypt in 606 BC and achieved political prominence in the Middle East. The bear stands for the Media-Persian Empire. The Media-Persians conquered the Babylonians in about 539 BC, and ruled until 331 BC when Alexander the Great defeated them (Daniel 8:21). The leopard represents the Greek Empire under Alexander which splintered into four separate kingdoms as Daniel prophesied it would (Daniel 8:8, 22). Four of Alexander's generals ruled over the divided empire: *Selencus* controlled the eastern provinces of Syria and Babylon, *Lysimachus* the northern regions of Asia Minor, *Ptolemy* possessed the southern countries including Egypt, and *Cassander* had the western parts, Greece, and adjacent territories. The last of these kingdoms survived until 31 BC, when as Daniel prophesied (Daniel 8:9-12, 23-25), the Roman Empire rose to power.

From this historical review, one may infer that the phrase "coming out of the sea" has to do with an empire or nation that is culturally and ethnically diverse. In Daniel's account, a succession of ethnic peoples from different geographic bases conquered one another, bringing together people from the continents of Africa, Asia, and Europe into a great mixture of customs, cultures, and languages.

As a nation of immigrants, *the United States fits this prophetic description.* Europeans and Africans joined indigenous peoples of North America during the colonial period, followed by waves of immigrants from all parts of the earth in the 19th and 20th centuries. Together, these peoples make up the American Nation.

America is known as a "Nation of Nations." The peopling of America is one of the great dramas in all human history. Over the years a massive stream of humanity—45 million people—crossed every ocean and continent to reach the United States. They came speaking many languages and representing most every nationality, race, and religion. Today, there are more people of Irish ancestry in the United States than in Ireland, more Jews than in Israel, more blacks than in most African countries. There are more people of Polish ancestry in Detroit than in most of the leading cities in Poland, and more than twice as many people of Italian ancestry in New York as in Venice.

The "melting pot" was once a popular image of American assimilation, but is now a disdained concept. The largest single ethnic strain is of European ancestry, approximately 70.5%. But the ethnic mix is so great, the relative contributions of different peoples are hard to determine. Estimations are German 20%, Irish 17%, English 16%, Scots 7%, other European 10.5%. Afro-Americans make up an estimated 12.1%, Hispanic 9.4%, Asian/ Pacific 3%, Jews, Arabs, Armenian and Iranian 4.2%, Native American 0.8%.[2]

The setting in which the history of all these people unfolded is no less impressive than the numbers and varieties of the peoples themselves. The United States is the largest cultural-linguistic unit in the world. The distance from San Francisco to Boston is the same as from Madrid to Moscow. Yet, here there is one primary language, one set of federal laws, and one economy. This same area in Europe is fragmented into a multitude of nations, languages, and competing military and political blocs.

Ten Horns

Understanding the biblical use of the words *"ten horns"* requires an interpretation of "ten," a number, and "horns," the characteristic of an animal. Ten needs the least explanation, although it represents something other than a count of 10.

Many of the numbers used in Scripture have symbolic meaning as well as their numerical value; Bible scholars have produced entire books on these meanings. From their study it is possible to say that "ten" denotes *all encompassing, order, and completeness.* Examples of Bible tens include the Ten Commandments, the ten virgins, and the ten plagues.

"Horns" needs a little more explanation. Throughout the Bible, a horn is emblematic of power and authority. As it is used in this verse, and in the book of Daniel, the word "horns" represents nations. These are nations with power and influence, but less power and influence than the beast-superpower to which they are associated. For the beast to have "ten horns" suggests that the beast has influence over several other powerful nations.

The United States is a power of superpower status. There are other powerful nations (horns). Several nations in the United Nations, for example, can be said to be powerful within a particular sphere of influence. Japan and Germany are economic powers; Russia is still a military power. France and England are former colonial powers that continue to hold political influence over other nations. But only the United States can claim to be a superpower. It exercises a certain amount of control over all these lesser powers, economic, military, and political. Perhaps the former Soviet Union had achieved superpower status, but now the United States stands alone. There is only one nation with a heavy influence over most other powerful nations qualifying it to meet John's prophecy of having "ten horns."

Another interpretation of "ten horns" holds that the horns represent European nations allied in the European Common Market (ECM). This amounts to speculation because it rests on the numerical and not the symbolic meaning of ten. As the phrase "ten horns" appears in Scripture, it is not limited to a number of nations that add up to ten. In Revelation 12:3, John uses "ten horns" to describe the Roman Empire, and historically, the Romans have been found to have controlled more than two dozen other nations.

In addition, to believe that "ten horns" refers to the ECM requires that exactly ten nations hold membership, no more, no less. The interpretation is only as stable as the ECM membership. To believe that ten means "all encompassing" and "horns" means regional powers does not require maintaining a count of ten nations as in the European Common Market. It simply requires acknowledgment of America's role as a superpower.

Seven Heads

"Seven heads" can be understood in a similar way as "ten horns." Bible scholars have determined that the number seven represents *complete or full* when it appears in Scripture. The word "head" refers to leadership. To apply the term "seven heads" to the end-time beast, would be to say that the superpower enjoys hegemony—superiority in all spheres of world leadership and influence. In other words, the superpower is "super" because it leads the world in commerce, agriculture, industry, military might, and so on.

Note that "seven heads" does not necessarily mean seven aspects of leadership—commerce, agriculture, and so on. It means that the last days empire has achieved full or complete leadership. The superpower dominates world affairs in whatever aspect of international influence is at hand.

Some have surmised that Russia, or the former Soviet Union, is the end-time power John describes. The collapse of the former Soviet Union weakens this argument, although it is true that Russia still exercises control over several other nations and retains significant military capability. Neither the former Soviet Union nor the Russia of today fits the "seven horns" description as well as the United States. Only America possesses superior strength in every aspect of world leadership. The United States is the sole superpower with "seven heads"—"complete leadership"—being number one in all areas.

Ten Crowns on His Horns

The word "crown" (or "diadem" as some versions read) was a distinctive mark of royalty among the early Greeks and Romans. As used by John in reference to the beast, it would mean governmental political control, or rather, the absence of it. When John writes that the crowns were positioned on the horns, meaning each country has its own governing political body, he indicates that the nations under the beast-superpower's influence retain political autonomy. John prophesies by this phrase that the last days empire has great influence over the other nations, but this influence does not include political control. That was not the case with the Roman Empire. In writing about the Roman Empire in Revelation 12:3, John states that the crowns (governing body) were located on the heads (Roman leadership) rather than the horns (individual nations). So Rome controlled other nations by political means, but the beast of Revelation 13 controls other nations by other than political means. This phrase, *"ten crowns on his horns,"* represents one of the most interesting and significant characteristics of the end-time superpower.

This imagery of crowns and horns, of politics and nations, is a telling description of America's relationship with other countries. America's influence stretches across the globe. Missionaries journeying to the remotest parts of the earth have found that American brand names, television programs, and popular music have preceded them. The United States maintains more military bases and foreign embassies than any other nation, and its technological, industrial, and commercial influence pull even more of the world's peoples into its grasp. Yet none of these people owe allegiance to the American flag; few of those under American influence are actually citizens of the United States.

How aptly John's phrase of crowns and horns describes American influence; the nations are heavily influenced by American culture and commerce, but not ruled by American law and government.

On Each Head a Blasphemous Name

In order to appreciate the significance of this phrase, "on each head a blasphemous name," it is necessary to understand blasphemy, because without a proper understanding of this sin, it is impossible to comprehend how it relates to the heads or aspects of the beasts' leadership.

Throughout the Old Testament, blasphemy was one of the gravest sins. To blaspheme is to make light of, or sport of God's sovereignty. In the New Testament, the Greek word used for blasphemy means "to injure one's reputation." It signifies irreverent speaking about God, or the use of God's holy name for an unholy purpose. An example can be found in Revelation 2:9 which reads, *"I know the blasphemy of them which say they are Jews, and are not, but are the synagogue of Satan"* (KJV). These wicked men blasphemed a sacred name when they labeled themselves Jews.

Another way to understand blasphemy is to think about what happened prior to the crucifixion of Christ. The Jewish high priests, elders, and teachers condemned Jesus to death for what they claimed was blasphemy. When Jesus acknowledged his deity, these religious leaders claimed he had misused the name of God. The Jewish leaders denied the deity of Christ, and therefore, Jesus' pronouncement was blasphemy to them because they knew that to say something unholy of God is to blaspheme.

The blasphemous name on each head that John speaks of in describing the beast of Revelation 13 would refer to a misuse of the sacred name of God. John indicates that in each area of leadership, each head, the last-days empire will use the sacred name of God to carry out unrighteous acts.

As applied to the United States, this would mean that the government promotes a worldly cause but claims an association with the name of God. This is, in fact, what happens today. The United States claims to be a Christian nation, yet it promotes evil, not good. The government promotes promiscuity in schools, sponsors the destruction of millions of unborn babies, and condones immoral, selfish life-styles. Yet the government continues to mint coins with the statement "In God We Trust," which is not true. This fits the Scriptural definition of blasphemy.

Undoubtedly, many of this nation's founders submitted to the Lord's direction. But on the way to worldwide superiority, America abandoned its founding principles. Other governments, other peoples, engage in wicked activities. But no other nation claims to have God's blessing while its people commit such great evil.

The United States Government fits all six of the characteristics John speaks of in Revelation 13:1. If this verse had been written in contemporary English, and the symbols were replaced with their contemporary explanation, it would read something like this:

And I saw a world superpower develop from the people of many nationalities. It influenced many other powerful nations throughout the world; it held a position of superiority in every area of world affairs, although it did not rule these other countries in a political sense; they governed themselves. It used the name of God freely and irreverently in many of its worldly activities.

>─┼◄►─○─◄►┼◄

QUICK REFERENCE OF WORDS AND PHRASES IN REVELATION 13:1

WORD OR PHRASE	PROPHETIC MEANING
Beast	Empire or superpower.
Out of the sea	A nation comprised of peoples with diverse cultural and ethnic background.
Numeral ten	Denotes all encompassing, order and completeness.
Horns	Nations with significant power, authority and influence, but not a superpower.
Numeral seven	Complete or full.
Heads	Refers to leadership.
Crowns or diadem	A distinct mark of royalty or governmental political control.
Ten crowns on his horns	Political control is maintained by the government of each nation, even though it is heavily influenced by the beast.
Blasphemy	To injure one's reputation; to use the name of God irreverently for an unholy purpose.
Each head a blasphemous name	Each area of leadership of the beast misuses the sacred name of God.

CHAPTER TWO

REVELATION 13:2

The beast I saw resembled a leopard, but had feet
like those of a bear and a mouth like that of a lion.
The dragon gave the beast his power and his
throne and great authority.

John continues his description of the last days beast-superpower. He refers to a lion, a bear, and a leopard; and a dragon who gives the beast his power, throne, and great authority. The symbolic animals can be readily understood from earlier discussion; the dragon's power, throne and authority require more extensive discussion. They refer to living in this world, one of the most widely discussed topics in Scripture.

Lion, Bear, and Leopard

Both John and Daniel use the names of these three animals to describe their visions. Daniel characterizes a different world power with each animal. The lion stands for the Babylonian Empire, the bear for the Media-Persian Empire, and the leopard for the Greek Empire. John, however, uses all three of these animals to describe a single empire. The lion, the bear, and the leopard describe the same nation—a nation that becomes the greatest superpower on the face of the earth.

In John's prophecy each animal portrays a facet of the end-time empire's strength. The leopard symbolizes military power and quickness. The superpower has the capacity to strike with speed and cunning. The bear symbolizes brute force, and the lion symbolizes power as well, but adds the element of pride in this nation's world leadership and conquest. The people of this nation relish their position of superiority. John says it is not just a mighty nation but a proud, boastful, haughty nation, and he affirms an important identifying characteristic.

Are the American people a meek, humble people who conduct their affairs out of a reverent fear of God? Or are they a conceited, arrogant people, quick to cheer "We're Number One!" at every opportunity? Sadly, I think the answer is clear.

The Dragon Gave the Beast His Throne, Power, and Authority

In Revelation 12:9 John states that the dragon is none other than Satan himself. From other Scriptures it is possible to identify what it means to give the beast-superpower his throne, power, and authority.

Satan's Throne

Satan is the god of this world. *"The god of this age (world) has blinded the minds of unbelievers"* (II Corinthians 4:4).

The Greek word translated as "world" is *kosmos*. As it is used in Scripture, *kosmos* or "world" has three primary meanings. **First,** "world" refers to the material universe (including the earth) as in Matthew 13:35. **Second,** "world" refers to the inhabitants of the earth, or mankind, as in John 3:16. **Third,** "world" is used to mean the cultural and social systems which bond humans together, otherwise known as "human society." Society is that realm of the world developed through human effort. It consists of religions; political structures and governments; economic, business, and financial systems; educational systems; science and technology; along with entertainments and amusements. Eliminate these things and you eliminate a society.

This **third** use of the word *"world"* is that which Satan controls. *It is his throne.* Since Adam and Eve ate the forbidden fruit, society has been made up of systems created by people. God gave

Adam and Eve authority over all of human society—the things they created. But when they disobeyed God, all of human society fell under the control of Satan. Since then, all societies on the face of the earth have been hostile to God.

The *world*, or what we call society, is Satan's throne. Society—those aspects of the world created by human effort—is under the control of Satan. *"We know that we are children of God, and the whole world (society) is under the control of the evil one (Satan)"* (I John 5:19). Satan rules the earth from his throne, the world, the social system he has built for himself. Notice how much easier it is to believe that there are evil things in our society, rather than that society itself is evil. Yet the Bible clearly teaches that society is evil, and the Evil One controls it.

As for you, you were dead in your transgressions and sins, in which you used to live when you followed the ways of this world and the ruler of the kingdom of the air, the spirit who is now at work in those who are disobedient. (Ephesians 2:1-2)

Unless converted, people are trapped in an unregenerate or spiritually lost state. They are not in God's family spiritually, but under Satan's influence. Therefore, unless God intervenes, all things which humans develop in their fallen spiritual condition fall under the realm of Satan's influence.

But this is not to say that societal things cannot be removed from Satan's system and claimed for the glory of God. Just as the inhabitants of the world can be converted, so too can the things they construct. Satan's authority over the world is limited by God's providential guidelines (see the Book of Job). Satan rules to the extent God allows him to. Satan has his limits. But on the whole, God's Word is clear that the systems and things developed by man that make up society (Satan's throne) are controlled by him and are often used as his elements to attack God's people in spiritual warfare.

Scripture About Satan's Throne—The World

The word "world" appears more than two hundred times in Scripture. It appears more often than the Holy Spirit, more often than love. Surely it is important for believers to understand Bible teaching on living in the world.

The Bible teaches that it is impossible to live both as a friend of the world and in God's family. *"You adulterous people, don't you know that friendship with the world is hatred toward God? Anyone who chooses to be a friend of the world becomes an enemy of God"* (James 4:4).

There are only two spiritual powers in the world. There is Satan, who promotes self-centeredness—seeking for "self"—and there is the Holy Spirit, who empowers believers to obey God's will. Both desire our inner being. Each person chooses which to be influenced by; no one can choose not to be influenced. It's one or the other.

In order to choose the Spirit of God, a person must separate from the world. Christians should not become attached to the things of the world. As John writes:

Do not love the world or anything in the world. If anyone loves the world, the love of the Father is not in him. For everything in the world—the cravings of sinful man (lust of the flesh), the lust of his eyes and the boasting of what he has and does (pride of life)—comes not from the Father but from the world. (I John 2:15-16)

Jesus instructs his followers to live in the world without being worldly.

My prayer is not that you take them out of the world but that you protect them from the evil one. They are not of the world, even as I am not of it. (John 17:15-16)

We are to keep ourselves unspotted from the world.

Religion that God, our Father accepts as pure and faultless is this: to look after orphans and widows in their distress and to keep oneself from being polluted (spotted) by the world. (James 1:27)

Separation cannot be accomplished without God's help. Christians must depend on God to build resistance to worldly influences. As Paul writes in Ephesians:

Finally, be strong in the Lord and in his mighty power. Put on the full armor of God so that you can take your stand against the devil's schemes. For our struggle is not against flesh and blood, but against the rulers, against the authorities, against the powers of this dark world and against the spiritual forces of evil in the heavenly realms. (Ephesians 6:10-12)

The Apostle Paul explains the believer's reliance on God this way: *"Do not conform any longer to the pattern of this **world**, but be transformed by the renewing of your mind"* (Romans 12:2). Then, Paul says, *". . . you will be able to test and approve what God's will is."*

There are some Christians who seem to have difficulty understanding who runs the order of societies. They attribute only a minor influence in the order of things to Satan and like to think this accurately describes his position. There seems to be a constant temptation in our minds to deny the possibility that Satan controls societies, regardless of what Scripture teaches.

Satan's Authority Over the World

Luke 4:1-13 describes the temptation of Christ. Notice what is said about the world:

The devil led him (Jesus) up to a high place and showed him in an instant all the kingdoms of the world. And he said to him, "I will give you all their

authority and splendor, for it has been given to
me, and I can give it to anyone I want to. So if you
worship me, it will all be yours." (Luke 4:5-7)

Satan claimed to own the world, and Jesus did not dispute his claim. Jesus knew that Satan has authority over the world. He is called "the ruler of this world" eight times in Scripture; some translations include the phrase "prince of the world," but the meaning is the same.

The Beast-Superpower Receives Satan's Throne, Power, and Authority

It is as we understand Satan's position of power and authority in the societies of this world that we will understand John's statement in Revelation 13:2 about Satan giving the beast-superpower his authority and power over his throne, the **world**. For Satan to give a world superpower his authority and power over his throne would allow that superpower to gain for itself superlative status in the "elements of a society that make up the world"—the position of number one in economics, military strength, politics, industry, agriculture, production of goods and services, etc. The United States definitely meets the criteria of this identifying characteristic. We have held the number one position in the world in every category since World War II.

The United States Government made a leap in its "world position" after World War I. After World War II, when similar conditions existed, the United States emerged as the most prosperous and mighty of all nations. It became a world superpower which no other country was in a position to challenge. As John prophesied, we received the throne of Satan's kingdom, "the world," a superpower rising up in the center of Christianity.

Historical records prove it was primarily the outcome of World War II that allowed our country to become the leading world power, far surpassing all other countries in all areas that make up our world society. This was not our position before World War II. This position developed for the United States because other leading powers had both their military and economic strength destroyed in World War II, while ours was actually enhanced. Other powerful countries lost a large number of their fighting forces. This alone seriously affected the structure and strength of those countries. So when we consider that all the fighting was done on the soil of the other leading world powers, destroying many of their industrial complexes, cities, farms, and homes, we can begin to realize why we emerged as the world's leader—a beast with seven heads. We were in a position to supply the world with most of its goods and services after World War II, which developed a wealth in our nation beyond one's imagination.

A book could be written about our government gaining the throne of the world and its political, economic, military, industrial, and other benefits. As in verse one, the United States Government is the only superpower which meets these distinct identifying characteristics John gives in verse two. We *have* been given a position in the world of power, on the throne, having great authority.

This relationship between the dragon, the beast, and the beast's authority will become clearer with a look at the next few verses in which John provides more information about how the beast acquired its power.

>-+-●-●-+-◄

CHAPTER THREE

REVELATION 13:3

One of the heads of the beast seemed to have had a fatal wound, but the fatal wound had been healed. The whole world was astonished and followed the beast.

In the first two verses of this chapter, John provides descriptive characteristics of the end-times superpower. In this verse, he prophesies about a particular event—recovery from a mortal wound. Specifically, John says four things about this monumental event:

1. One of the beast's heads (areas of leadership) receives the fatal wound. Or, in other words, one (please note only *one*) aspect of the superpower's superiority is nearly wiped out.

2. The wounded head heals. This aspect of the superpower recovers.

3. The world is amazed at this recovery. The recovery is dramatic, awesome, and inexplicable.

4. After the wound heals, the world follows the beast. The wound and its recovery catapults the superpower to a position of leadership in the world.

What John does not say in this verse is which head suffered the wound and recovered. He does, however, provide the answer in verse 14 in which he tells how the beast was wounded.

The second half of Revelation 13:14 reads: *". . . He ordered them to set up an image in honor of the beast who was wounded by the sword and yet lived."* In biblical times the phrase "wounded by the sword," which reveals the source of the beast's wound, indicates military action. It was a wound to the beast's military head. Or, in other words, the mortal wound that heals has to do with the superpower's military leadership. When the last-days empire regained its military might after nearly losing it altogether, the empire is elevated to its superior position of leadership in the world as never before.

As I have explained in verses 1 and 2, the United States Government is the beast. But in order for this interpretation to square with Scripture, it must also fit verse 3. Few today would doubt the military superiority of the United States. But if the American Government is the beast, then this military capability must be *severely wounded,* then emerge on the world stage in such a dramatic turn of events that the other nations of the world are astonished.

It also follows that if the United States is today the superpower referred to in verses 1 and 2, then this event must have *already occurred.* Something in this nation's past must match the description of a mortal military wound for the prophecy to fit. To put it in the form of a question: When did the United States become a superpower? Or, to be more specific: What historical event involving the United States military led to the development of this nation becoming the world's greatest superpower?

To find the answer requires some thinking about American history. The event must have occurred within the last hundred years or so, because at the time of the Civil War and before, Americans fought with themselves to decide whether there would be an America. The event could not have occurred within the last few decades, though, because the United States had already become a superpower. America forced the Soviet Union to back down in 1962, and had made agreements with its World War II allies over which portions of the earth it would control even before the war ended. The wound and its recovery must have occurred during the early twentieth century.

Certainly, both world wars were watershed events for the United States. World War I saw the United States involved in global conflict, but the thrust of its foreign policy was geared toward this hemisphere. The United States Government limited its international influence to Central America and the Caribbean. It was during World War II, the 1940s, that the United States became a power with globe-encircling interests. American influence in Africa, Asia, Europe, and the Middle East accompanied the Cold War. It is unnerving to realize how closely the event that led to United States involvement in World War II matches John's prophecy of the beast, the end-time superpower, receiving a mortal wound to its military leadership.

History records the event happening on December 7, 1941. On that day, millions of Americans huddled around their radios to hear the news. Confusion, shock, and disbelief spread across the nation. The lives of the American people had been thrown into turmoil and fear. America had been attacked for the first time in over a century, and we were at war. It seemed impossible! News of war ignited a frenzy of activity in the months that followed as a nation mobilized its resources. Victory gardens sprung up, recycling bins appeared, and gas rationing cards were used. Factories that produced autos were converted to produce airplanes, boats, and tanks. There was no escape from talk of war. The unthinkable had happened. The Japanese had bombed Pearl Harbor.

The Wound of the Beast

The Japanese attack on Pearl Harbor is the most significant naval operation in twentieth century military history. But it was even more than that—it was one of the turning points in modern world history. This "day of infamy" was the catalytic event of the century. It was so sudden, so spectacular, so devastating. So much happened that day—militarily, politically, and psychologically. Many people who lived through the 1900s tend to divide their lives into two periods—before Pearl Harbor and after Pearl Harbor.

It is difficult to exaggerate the importance of naval power prior to the Nuclear Age. During the 1940s and earlier, most Americans believed, as did people throughout the industrialized world, that ships represented the ultimate technological achievement. Battle-ships were the mightiest weapons of war, and luxury liners repre-sented the epitome of western culture. The sinking of great ships—the *Lusitania*, the *Bismarck*, the *Titanic*—inspired legends and ballads. Sinking ships were cataclysmic events akin to natural disasters like earthquakes and hurricanes. At Pearl Harbor, the United States lost nineteen ships in a matter of hours.

Prelude to Pearl Harbor

In the spring of 1940, a large segment of America's Pacific Fleet had been stationed at Pearl Harbor. It was the world's greatest aggregation of warships—a million tons of fighting steel—and it secured the western front of our mighty nation.

United States influence in the Pacific irritated the Japanese. Japan feared that America's huge naval program threatened Japan's ambitious career of conquest in the 1930s. While the European nations fought each other, Japan built its empire in Southeast Asia. The island nation could not miss this golden opportunity.

The Japanese planned to strike a fatal blow to the United States Pacific Fleet. It was the American naval fleet, situated at Pearl Harbor, that stymied Japan's conquest of Southeast Asia. The Japa-nese were confident they could deal with British and Dutch naval forces, and withstand an American counterattack, but only if the Pacific Fleet was out of the way. They seized upon a plan by Admiral Isoroku Yamamoto, Commander-in-Chief of Japan's combined fleet. He urged the Japanese Imperial Council to make use of their aircraft carriers to carry out a crippling attack.

He reasoned that if Japan were to achieve political supremacy in the Pacific, it would have to neutralize America's military capac-ity. Yamamoto knew that just as a weaker judo expert can toss a stronger opponent by catching him off balance, Japan would have to seize the initiative for the island nation to defeat the United States. By knocking out the United States Pacific Fleet in one bold stroke, Yamamoto hoped to gain the edge in military strength for a year. He and his advisors concluded that Japan could best achieve an early decisive engagement with the United States Navy by bringing the scene of action to the waters of the Hawaiian Islands. Yamamoto's plan was to catch the United States sleeping—literally.

For more than a year, the naval forces of the Rising Sun carried out steady, careful preparations. All of the planning had to be done in the strictest secrecy. The attack would have to catch the United States by surprise or it would fail. Japanese military planners had to solve several problems in order to launch the attack. They designed torpedoes capable of operating in the shallow waters of Pearl Harbor; they produced new armor-piercing shells that could be delivered by planes flying at low altitudes; they selected pilots and trained them to fly in an area like Pearl Harbor. The Japanese also had to organize the task force, learn how to refuel the ships in the rough northern Pacific Ocean—the route selected to avoid detection—and choose the best day and time for the attack to assure a complete surprise. The Pearl Harbor plan was the most highly-classified, closely-guarded, best-kept secret of World War II.

Pearl Harbor Day

At 6 o'clock on the morning of November 26, 1941, the Japanese strike force weighed anchor. Twelve days later they reached the launching point for their attack: 230 miles due north of the island of Oahu, Hawaii. It was just before dawn on December 7. The Japanese force of 33 warships included six aircraft carriers that had successfully sailed on a northern route through rough waters and dense fog to avoid detection by American ships and surveillance aircraft.

On every Japanese carrier that Sunday morning the scene was the same. As aircraft engines sputtered to life, plane after plane rose in the sky, flashing in the early morning sun that peeked over the horizon. This airborne armada consisted of 353 planes. It represented the largest concentration of air power in the history of warfare. On the island of Oahu, American sailors were unaware of the tremendous fighting force that would send many of them to a watery grave.

Perfect timing was essential. The Japanese knew full well that if anything went wrong, the entire surprise attack would collapse. They were now dead on course. Their mission: destruction of the United States Pacific Fleet at Pearl Harbor and all of the nearby American Air Force installations. The first bombs fell just before 8 o'clock a.m. Japanese pilots, operating from six aircraft carriers, targeted air and naval bases. They flew at treetop level; each wave brought massive destruction. The element of surprise belonged to the Japanese.

In less than two hours, the Japanese had immobilized almost the entire air strength of Oahu and nearly eliminated their chief objective, the United States Pacific Fleet. The once mighty United States military fortress at Oahu had been pulverized. Wreckage floated across the oily surface of the water; bodies washed ashore. Steam hissed, flames crackled. Half-submerged ships strewn about the harbor tilted at crazy angles. As the billows of black smoke over Oahu began to clear, United States forces assessed the damage. Yamamoto's forces had sunk four battleships, and severely damaged four others. Eleven other warships had been sunk or immobilized, and more than *340 American aircraft* had been destroyed. Japanese losses totalled 29 aircraft.

The Japanese operation at Pearl Harbor was a stroke of military genius incomparable to any other in the history of warfare. The United States had suffered one of the greatest defeats any nation ever endured at the beginning of a war. The Japanese secured mastery of the Far East in a couple of hours. In Germany, news of the defeat tempted Hitler to declare war on the United States. In the aftermath, the congressional committee convened to investigate the event filled 40 volumes with its findings.

The Fatal Wound Heals

The event that December morning was even more than a stunning military operation. Historians, statesmen, and journalists throughout the world refer to this attack as one of the greatest turning points in the history of the modern world. At the time, the world viewed the event as a mortal wound to United States military leadership. The attack roused the fighting spirit of Americans, however, as nothing else could. During the next three and a half years, the United States forged a war machine that conquered enemy forces in European and Asian theaters. It transformed the United States from a provincial, regional power to a technological, military, and political titan stretching across both hemispheres and changed forever the American way of life.

The Legacy of Pearl Harbor

As the inhabitants of the choicest piece of real estate on earth, the American people have always enjoyed a level of material prosperity greater than many others. Yet, the United States really became a prosperous, influential nation only after World War II, when Americans standard of living leaped forward at a faster pace than any nation in the world. In the years immediately after the war, the economy sputtered. Wartime production fell, as did the hopes of many Americans, who feared a second Great Depression. But during the 1950s, national income doubled, and it nearly doubled again during the 1960s.

Americans achieved this unprecedented level of prosperity because World War II enhanced American fortunes. Nations of Europe and Asia, powerful before the war, were ravaged by its devastation. Years of fighting had razed their cities, tattered their industries, and robbed them of a generation of their best and brightest young people. None of the fighting had occurred on American soil, so the United States emerged as the only power with its industrial base intact. This put American factories in a unique position to furnish its wartime allies with many of the products and services their people needed. During the next thirty years, United States exports fueled a fantastic economic boom which gave the American people the highest standard of living in the world.

The Arizona Memorial - The Wound Remembered

When President Bush visited Pearl Harbor on the 50th anniversary of the Japanese attack, he saw the battleship USS Arizona

USS Arizona

resting in an upright position under 38 feet of water. Hit by a single 1760 pound action bomb on that awful

day, the Arizona sank in less than nine minutes. The bomb pen-
etrated through six decks of steel and exploded in the main avia-
tion fuel storage tank. The force of the explosion was so tremendous that it raised the bow of the ship completely out of the water,
and split it right behind the number one gun turret. Of the 1543
crew members aboard, 1177 perished in those few minutes.

The years have slipped by quickly, and the scars of the attack
have all but been forgotten by most Americans. However, the stark
horror and grim reminder of defeat that Sunday morning which
caught the country in
the fierce vortex of
history will live for-
ever through the
Arizona Memorial.

**Memorial
Spans
Sunken
USS Arizona**

Today, the sunken
Arizona pays tribute
to the fury of defeat
on Pearl Harbor Day and the 1100 men still entombed in its rust-
ing hull. On Memorial Day 1962, the government opened a float-
ing memorial. Visitors stand atop the wreckage to look down at
the remains of the sunken ship, resting quietly at the bottom of Pearl
Harbor. It is astounding to discover that the theme of the design used for building this memorial matches John's prophecy
in Revelation 13:3 of the beast's fatal wound that is healed.

The memorial was designed with a sag in the middle. Solid
white walls and roof comprise two ends of the rectangular-shaped
building, exposing a thin archway of bare, white ribs. The depressed
center was purposely designed to express the initial wound to a great
nation and the sturdy ends to express its eventual recovery and
victory. The United States jumped to its feet, despite the wound

Arizona
Memorial
Design
Theme

that had cut the heart out of its military, to present the most fearsome warrior the world had ever known.

After World War II, our country emerged as the greatest political, military, industrial, and economic power ever to exist on the face of the earth. We, indeed, had received the throne of the world as John prophesied in verse two. This was soon proven as many countries aligned themselves with the United States Government. The entire world was awestruck by the way the United States demonstrated its great power and ended the war with the dropping of the atomic bomb. *"The fatal wound had indeed been healed,"* as stated by John.

CHAPTER FOUR

REVELATION 13:4

*Men worshipped the dragon because he had given
authority to the beast, and they also worshipped
the beast and asked, "Who is like the beast? Who
can make war against him?"*

Worship means to serve, venerate, or hold in awe. In this verse,
John describes the attitude of the people on the earth toward the
last-days empire. The phrases *"Who is like the beast? Who can make
war against him?"* indicate military might without equal. John foretells of the time after the beast recovers, when the nation demonstrates awesome military power, and commands the respect and fear
of peoples throughout the world.

The United States achieved this distinction on July 16, 1945,
when scientists working near an old ranch house outside
Alamogordo, New Mexico, detonated the first atomic bomb. Yankee technological know-how and industrial might advanced scien-
tific knowledge beyond anything that had gone on before. At 5:30
in the morning, American and exiled European scientists triggered
humanity's first nuclear weapon of war. With a blinding flash of
light, a wave of heat ripped past the observers as they watched a
giant mushroom cloud rise above the desert that day.

On August 6, 1945, an aircraft blessed by a Catholic priest dropped an atomic bomb on the City of Hiroshima. People and buildings became a black, boiling mass. Survivors of the blast wandered the streets in tattered clothes crying out for water. Seventy thousand people died in five minutes. Countless more died from burns and cancer in the next few months. Three days later, the United States dropped a second bomb on Nagasaki. Another 80,000 died instantly. Japan surrendered unconditionally, pleading only for the emperor to remain on his throne.

Why Truman decided to make the United States the only country in world history to use a nuclear weapon during a war remains something of a mystery. Marshall, Eisenhower, and MacArthur believed nuclear weapons to be unnecessary. Japan's war machine teetered on the brink of collapse, its factories idled for want of raw materials, its people starving on less than subsistence rations. But one truth is clear. Americans exacted revenge on the Japanese for the humiliation at Pearl Harbor. One nation alone possessed the power to convert cities into ashes and shadows, and the other nations of the world took notice. "America stands at this moment," said Winston Churchill in 1945, "at the summit of the world."

The attitude that prevailed after World War II, which John prophetically calls an attitude of worship or to "hold in awe," certainly describes the world's thinking after America defeated both Japan and Germany. Few would question the prophecy given in this verse. And still today, regardless of what people around the world think of the United States, they stand in awe of our life-style and of our world leadership position.

>-+*>-0-<*-+-<

CHAPTER FIVE

REVELATION 13:5-6

The beast was given a mouth to utter proud words and blasphemies and to exercise his authority for forty-two months. He opened his mouth to blaspheme God, and to slander his name and his dwelling place and those who live in heaven.

In these two verses, the beast engages in three activities: (1) "to utter proud (haughty) words," (2) "to exercise authority for forty-two months," and (3) "to blaspheme God." Each of these can be understood in turn.

To Utter Proud Words
Haughtiness means a feeling of promotion of self as being better than others. It means to display pride in personal accomplishments. The American people are a proud people, taking great pride in their worldly position, accomplishments, and conquests. God hates this attitude (Proverbs 6:16-17).

To Exercise Authority for 42 Months
In the second verse of this chapter, John says that the beast receives three worldly positions: power, worldly throne, and great *authority*. In verses 5 and 6, he explains that the superpower makes use of this authority for a period of time, "forty-two months," in

John's words. While doing so, the beast utters blasphemies or irreverently uses the name of God, that is, it declares that its position of worldly authority was God given.

During this time, the United States assumes its superior position and uses this superiority to commit terrible evil. Yet, as the rest of this passage states, it will claim to act in God's name. The phrase "forty-two months" may be interpreted one of two ways.

1. *Forty-two months may refer to a nonspecific period of time.* Forty-two months, if taken literally, adds up to three and a half years. However, John may have used this expression of time in a figurative sense as is often done in prophecy. In the Hebrew tradition there are several phrases that are roughly equivalent to "awhile" in English—an indefinite period of time that lingers and lingers. One of these is the phrase *"a time, times and half a time,"* as in Revelation 12:14. If a "time" in this phrase is taken to mean one year, then "forty-two months" bears a resemblance because one year (12 months) plus two years (24 months) plus half a year (6 months) equals three and a half years (42 months).

2. *Forty-two months may refer to a specific period of time.* John may mean for this phrase to be understood literally as three and a half years. Perhaps this period of time has yet to begin; it will occur in the future. Perhaps it has started but has yet to end; we may be currently living during this period. Or, it may be that this time occurred at some point in the past. If it has already occurred, it reveals something interesting about the United States and its role as the beast.

Consider 42 months in reference to verse 2, in which the United States receives its worldly power and authority from Satan, and in reference to verse 3, which tells of the mortal wound, the defeat at Pearl Harbor. Four days after the bombing of Pearl Harbor, December 11, 1941, Germany (along with Italy and allies of Japan) declared war on the United States. On the same day, the United States returned the sentiment by a unanimous vote of the House and Senate. Germany surrendered on May 7, 1945. May 1945 was the forty-second month since December 1941, by using the Jewish calendar of thirty days per month; therefore, this is a meaningful date within the Jewish frame of reference.

Though the number of days does not equal the exact equivalent of forty-two months of thirty days, this does not invalidate the significance of "42 months" for the United States. As a first century Jewish man, John would not have measured time the way we do today.

Prior to the Industrial Revolution, people measured time in less exact terms. Solar cycles marked the passage of time, not clocks and calendars. A day, for example, meant the period of time from sunset to sunset, not 24 hours from midnight to midnight as we now measure a day. That Jesus died on a Friday afternoon and arose that following Sunday morning is consistent with the expression "three days," even though this period of times does not equal 72 hours.

It is also appropriate to apply "42 months" to the period of time the United States and Germany were at war, rather than that of the United States and Japan, because although the war with Japan was most significant to Americans, the war with Germany was the most significant to Jewish people. The United States continued its war in the Pacific after May 1945, but the holocaust ended with the defeat of Germany.

Blasphemous Words

Blasphemous words, as I have discussed, refer to the irreverent use of God's name. John says that the people who display the proud attitude will have a government that will be blasphemous in character. The end-time superpower will openly flaunt its position, superiority, and accomplishments. It will sponsor evil activities under the auspices of God's holy name.

An honest look at America's role during World War II reveals a nation that fits this prophecy. The United States Government claimed to have entered the war for a moral purpose. Congress insisted the war had been "thrust upon" the nation. President Roosevelt emphasized the date "which will live in infamy" to argue for an American response to unprovoked aggression. After the war, the United States used its influence across the world for what it claimed was a moral purpose. Many Americans cling to the belief that America emerged from the war in such a good position because of our national righteousness and collective trust in God.

But war has never resulted in the promotion of Christian interests and values. Throughout history, peoples that appear as conquerors emerge victorious because they commit acts of brutality, greed, and power. The United States is no exception. The United States involvement in this war was due to the age-old sins of self-centeredness, selfishness, and covetousness.

An abundance of information, including material located in State Department files, reveals that America's primary purpose for entry into World War II was to establish a stronger military and economic position in the world. It indicates that Roosevelt took no precautions against Japanese attack because he knew that retaliation against the Rising Sun would mean joining the war in Europe. He knew the treaty agreed to by Japan, Germany, and Italy would make all three countries enemies of the United States. The chief objective was the destruction of Germany, not Japan. Rear Admiral Robert A. Theobald wrote: "The fact that war with Japan meant war with Germany and Italy played an important part in President Roosevelt's diplomatic strategy. Throughout the approach to the war and during the fighting, the primary United States objective was the defeat of Germany."[1] Prime Minister Winston Churchill made a similar statement to Great Britain's House of Commons on January 27, 1942, that Roosevelt's strategy in using Japan was to get the United States involved in the war in Europe.

The United States used the war to extend its political and commercial interests across the globe. America occupied nations in western Europe and Asia after the war that were invaded by Germany and Japan during the war. Former British and French colonies became United States possessions. Industrial interests, along with the strength of our business community, coupled with hundreds of military bases, appeared in more than 50 foreign nations on every continent; and our navy patrolled every ocean. Military presence opened new markets for United States goods, and extraction of raw materials for American factories. To preserve its position, the United States Government has supported totalitarian regimes in Latin America, the Middle East, and elsewhere in the world.

Ultimately, the great powers of the world fought the Second World War to determine whether Germany would be the dominant power in Europe, and Japan in Asia, or whether the United States Government would be the dominant superpower throughout the world. The American cause was not to promote freedom and democracy for other peoples. If the United States dislikes totalitarian regimes, why has it allowed dictatorships in China, Eastern Europe, Latin America, and Southeast Asia?

Please understand what I am saying. I am not saying the believer should not serve in military forces or pursue a political career, nor am I saying that Christians should not respect civil authority or governing officials. God can use His people in many areas, and His people should allow the Spirit of God to lead them where He wills. I am saying that the United States Government's history of military conquest during World War II was not motivated by concern for promotion of Christian virtue.

Many American Christians, influenced by our communications media, believe that the foreign policy of the United States over the years has been mainly concerned with the extension of freedom to other peoples. Because of this teaching we have become somewhat blinded to the biblical teaching that governmental systems are of the world. Therefore, they generally serve a worldly purpose. This is not to say that they overrule God's providence, but they are often the vehicles used by Satan to attack and negatively influence God's standards and God's people.

Many Americans are now speaking of how the cultural and spiritual values in our country have fallen so low in just this last generation. This has all happened since we gained the throne of Satan's world. Though it may have appeared that as a nation we have been in the ideal world position, being number one in all things, spiritually this supremacy has taken its toll. We have become proud and haughty. It opened the door for our spiritual enemy to tear down our country's Christian heritage and destroy many of the biblical standards that most of the American people lived by. Since our government became the end-time beast-super-power over the world system at the end of World War II, we have lost many spiritual battles in our country, which is what John, in the next verse, prophesied would happen.

>-+-•>-0-•<+-+-<

CHAPTER SIX

REVELATION 13:7a

*He (the beast) was given power to make war
against the saints and to conquer them.*

John foretells the beast's—ultimately Satan's—fearsome power
over the people of God. He says that the world superpower will
"make war against the saints" and "conquer" or "overcome" God's
people. John is talking about a spiritual state of being. For God's
people to be conquered means for them to lose their discernment
about right and wrong. To comprehend how the United States fits
into this requires a closer look at the issues involved.

To Conquer the Saints

The word "conquer" brings to mind the defeat of one army by
another. This is, in fact, a good illustration because the word means
to overcome, defeat, or subdue—not obliterate or eliminate. The
United States used powerful nuclear weapons to conquer Japan, but
it did not eliminate Japan from the globe. Even after its defeat,
Japan continued to exist as a nation.

What John says, then, is that Satan will use the United States
Government to overwhelm, but not eliminate, Christians. The enemy will use American society to dull God's people into a spiritual
stupor. Christians will fail to live the normal Christian life, and
wonder why they lack spiritual power. They will be unable to see

41

Satan at the root of their problems. This is a good description of the spiritual condition of America today.

Satan is winning the war for the hearts and minds of Americans, and many Christians do not know enough to be concerned. Many cannot recognize the enemy's tactics and don't know what to expect from him. Those who have already been captured—and have surrendered many of their biblical ideas and standards to the worldly standards of the Evil One—do not know they have been victimized by spiritual deception. Often, they speak and act contrary to basic godly principles.

Many of God's people do not live out God's principles in their family and business relationships, entertainment desires and material needs. Defeated Christians have trouble recognizing Christian morality and values. Our apathy toward sin is a true barometer of this condition. Pastors, in addition to the many professional counseling organizations that have appeared in recent years, expend great resources to help needy Christians. Contemporary Christians seem as helpless to keep their families together as worldly people. For example, the divorce rate of over 50 percent in our society is nearly as high among Christians.

Despite the many ministries that are devoted to Christian service, the dedication of numerous pastors and teachers, and the sacrifice and hard work of many Christians in other areas, the fruit produced by our society in recent years reveals that we are losing the spiritual war for Christian standards in America. We are fulfilling the prophetic word in Revelation 13:7, the beast-system has been given power to make war against the saints and overcome them. Satan's beast-system has definitely influenced and affected the spiritual walk of most Christians which has caused us to often lose sight of what it means to lead a committed spiritual life. We know what to say in Christian circles to make it seem as if we are devoted, but our actions broadcast our weakness to the world. So many opportunities to grow in the knowledge of God are available to us in America today, yet the spirit of independence, self-gratification, and self-centeredness permeates God's people.

Does this mean that because John foretells a time when Satan's beast-system overcomes the saints, that Christians are powerless to resist? That there is no reason to attempt to stand up for what is right because the prophecy of defeat must be fulfilled? No, clearly not. Satan wields great power to be sure. His method of deception is an insidious and dangerous weapon. But individuals must fight. The fulfillment of this prophecy refers to a general state or condition that prevails. Conquering the saints does not mean that Satan will immobilize every individual. Speaking of the last days, Jesus says that the deception will be great, but not great enough to deceive everyone. *"For false Christs and false prophets will appear and perform great signs and miracles to deceive even the elect— if that were possible"* (Matthew 24:24).

How is the beast-system being used effectively to spiritually overcome many of the saints in their commitment to the teachings and standards of Scripture? In II Thessalonians, the Apostle Paul provides important insight into the spirit of lawlessness, the key to the beast's ability to conquer the saints in our day.

Spirit of Lawlessness: II Thessalonians 2:1-4

To understand Paul's message requires learning the meaning of some prophetic words used in these verses:

> *Concerning the coming of our Lord Jesus Christ and our being gathered to him, we ask you, brothers, not to become easily unsettled or alarmed by some prophecy, report or letter supposed to have come from us, saying that the day of the Lord has already come. Don't let anyone deceive you in any way, for that day will not come until the rebellion occurs and the man of lawlessness is revealed, the man doomed to destruction. (2 Thessalonians 2:1-3)*

Paul's opening statement, *"Concerning the coming of our Lord Jesus Christ and our being gathered to him,"* indicates that he is talking about the last days. Evidently, the Thessalonians (a body of believers living at Thessalonica) misunderstood the coming of Christ, and Paul warns them not to be fooled. Paul says that Jesus will not come until two things happen: *(1) the rebellion occurs and (2) the man of lawlessness is revealed.*

The Rebellion

The Greek word Paul uses for rebellion is apostasia. It means to defect or fall into apostasy, the abandonment or renunciation of belief in the standards of biblical Christianity. Paul tells believers through all the ages that Christ will not return before there is a rebellion or falling away. This state of rebellion characterizes the general state of the church—the Body of Christ—at the close of the Church Age.

Paul describes the attitude or spirit that develops within American society—the society that has been the center of Christian activity during the last days of the Church Age. Although many people profess Christianity and personal commitment to Christ, they refuse to obey God's Word. These rebels display no conscience against many sins of the world, no fear of God, no attachment to Scripture. They continue to wrap themselves in the trappings of religious service, but their commitment to obtain material possessions at the expense of spiritual commitment, the entertainment they seek, the life-styles they live out, reveal that they have abandoned the cause of Christ.

The Man of Lawlessness

It is those who rebel that Paul calls *the man of lawlessness.* The King James version reads *that man of sin, the son of perdition.* In modern English a more suitable phrase would be "lawless man." These phrases mean the same thing, and taken together, provide insight into the message Paul intends to communicate in these verses.

Among the early Jewish people, it was a custom to refer to someone who displayed a particular trait or characteristic as the "son of" that characteristic. So, since Paul refers here to those who engage in lawless behavior, he uses the phrase *son of perdition or man of lawlessness.* He describes a spirit of disbelief that sweeps through the center of Christianity during the end times and brings about the rejection of Christ-like standards.

Jesus spoke of this same condition of apostasy when he told the disciples: *"As it was in the days of Noah, so it will be at the coming of the Son of Man"* (Matthew 24:37). In Noah's day, people had lost the fear of the Lord, and lawlessness prevailed. They were *eating and drinking, marrying and giving in marriage* and knew nothing about the coming judgment. When the disciples asked about the signs indicating the end of the age, Jesus said that people would revisit the days before the flood.

It has been taught that the *man of lawlessness* refers to a person who becomes a ruler during the last days. But this interpretation does not fit because Paul speaks here of a general condition that affects many people, not just one person.

The Greek word translated as *man* in this verse is *anthropes*. This word appears often in the New Testament to mean mankind or everyone. Here are some examples. *"So that the man (anthropes) of God may be thoroughly equipped"* (2 Timothy 3:17). *"What is man (anthropes) that you are mindful of him?"* (Hebrews 2:6). *"So that by the grace of God he might taste death for everyone (anthropes)"* (Hebrews 2:9). *"Everyone (anthropes) should be quick to listen, slow to speak and slow to become angry"* (James 1:19). In the next verse of II Thessalonians 2, Paul provides additional details about the rebellion of man that occurs before Christ's return.

He opposes and exalts himself over everything that is called God or is worshipped, and even sets himself up in God's temple, proclaiming himself to be God. (2 Thessalonians 2:4)

This is a significant verse. In it, Paul describes (1) the basic characteristic of society that leads to the rebellion, and (2) he identifies how the rebellion will occur.

Origins of Rebellion

The word "he" at the beginning of this verse refers to the lawless man. Notice that the pronoun "himself" occurs three times. This defines the characteristic of the rebellion. Paul does not say the rebels will reject church attendance. He does not say they will renounce denominational affiliation or lose the appearance of Christianity. He says they will put their own self-serving interests (himself) above God's. They will in essence set themselves up as though they are God and believe that they are capable of making moral judgments for themselves through societal or personal values. This is how the beast-system will influence and conquer the saints.

The Place of Rebellion

Where will this rebellion, this falling away, occur? The United States. Paul indicates this in that he is discussing the nature or attitude that develops in a society which had been the center of Christianity near the end-times. The rebellion must take place in a society of strong Christian teaching. How could there be a "rebellion" or "falling away" from Christian standards if it were not the prominent religious teaching of that society? How can you fall from something if you were not there first? And we know he is talking about the last days—the second coming of Jesus—because he states that clearly in II Thessalonians 2:1.

Paul's prophecy concerns the United States because he is talking about the church, and America has been the center of Christian activity. The United States began as a Christian nation. But now it is a nation that carries the name of a Christian nation, but denies true Christianity. As Paul writes in II Timothy 3:1-5:

> *But mark this: There will be a terrible time in the last days. People will be lovers of themselves, lovers of money, boastful, proud, abusive, disobedient to their parents, ungrateful, unholy, without love, unforgiving, slanderous, without self-control, brutal, not lovers of the good, treacherous, rash, conceited, lovers of pleasure rather than lovers of God—having a form of godliness but denying its power.*

"Having a form of godliness but denying its power"—this is a telling phrase in relation to American Christianity. Those who claim to be members of God's family continue their religious activities,

yet the wickedness of American society reveals their weakened, pitiful state. American Christians claim little victory over many sins, and they often have no power over temptation, a power that can only come from walking in the power of the indwelling Holy Spirit.

There are those who say that this person in verse 4 who *"opposes and exalts himself… even sets himself up in God's Temple,"* refers to how some person, usually referred to as the anti-Christ, will appear in Jerusalem, the site of the Jewish temple. This teaching does not fit Paul's use of *anthropes* in verse 3 as discussed, nor does it fit the word he uses for rebellion, *apostasia*. It also does not square with the Greek word translated *temple* in this verse.

Two Greek words are translated "temple." One is *hieron* and usually refers to the temple in Jerusalem. The other is *naos*, and is used to refer to the heart of the temple in Jerusalem, but in Christianity it is the word used which refers to a believer as the temple of God. For example, *"Don't you know that you yourselves are God's temple (naos) and that God's Spirit lives in you?"* (I Corinthians 3:16). *"Do you not know that your body is a temple (naos) of the Holy Spirit, who is in you, whom you have received from God?"* (I Corinthians 6:19). *"For we are the temple (naos) of the living God"* (II Corinthians 6:16). *"In him the whole building is joined together and rises to become a holy temple (naos) to the Lord. And in him you too are being built together to become a dwelling in which God lives by his Spirit"* (Ephesians 2:21-22). In 2 Thessalonians 2:4 Paul uses the Greek word *naos* for temple. This demonstrates he had in mind the human body, not a building.

Paul is addressing Christians, and in Christianity mankind is the temple. He describes the body of a person in this verse, not a building used as a place of worship. He prophesies about how last-days Christians who fall away will do so as they are influenced to become self-serving to the extent they exalt and serve themselves above God. This, in essence, is the heart of the religion of humanism and is the power that the beast-system has to overcome the saints. This method of Satan's is very deceptive and similar to the attacks he used to deceive God's people throughout Scripture, beginning with Adam and Eve.

Temptation of Adam and Eve

To be counted among the elect who challenge Satan's domination, and not the rebels who abandon God's ways, we need to know how to combat Satan's current method of attack.

Genesis Chapter 3 reveals the devices Satan has used to deceive people throughout time. Satan's deception began in the Garden of Eden, when he wanted to break down the communication between God and His children. Tragically, he lulled the first two of the earth's inhabitants to fall from the state of grace, and through their sin, all of the people to follow were born into sin, having a sinful nature. But in this temptation Satan also revealed his strategy, his master-plan for conquering the earth. Satan's goal has not changed, neither has his strategy. The temptations and choices we meet everyday are displayed for us in this tragic story.

Now the serpent was more crafty than any of the wild animals the Lord God had made. He said to the woman, "Did God really say, 'You must not eat from any tree in the garden'? "

The woman said to the serpent, "We may eat fruit from the trees in the garden, but God did say, 'You must not eat fruit from the tree that is in the middle of the garden, and you must not touch it, or you will die.' "

"You will not surely die," the serpent said to the woman. "For God knows that when you eat of it your eyes will be opened, and you will be like God, knowing good and evil."

When the woman saw that the fruit of the tree was good for food and pleasing to the eye, and also desirable for gaining wisdom, she took some and ate it. She also gave some to her husband, who was with her, and he ate it. (Genesis 3:1-6)

Four of the techniques Satan uses to deceive people can be seen in these verses:

1. *He implants thoughts of doubt which can lead to outright denial of the meaning of God's Word.* Every day, every hour, the enemy raises doubts in our minds. He operates through many mediums to reach our reasoning and thinking—using television, other worldly entertainment media and even conversation with friends. If we are not alert and careful when thinking, viewing, and conversing, Satan, (as he did with Eve) leads the believer to wonder: "Does it really make a difference to God?" "God's Word really doesn't mean that, does it?"

If the believer confronts the doubt for what it is, then Satan is rebuffed. But if the doubt is not dealt with, Satan gains a foothold that he then uses to generate outright denial. "No, that doesn't really matter to God, it can't make that much difference." "No, the Bible is talking about something else." This kind of denial leads to disobedience, a break in our communion with God and spiritual defeat. And ultimately, if not corrected, to rejection of who God is.

Notice that Satan did not encourage Eve to reject God altogether. Instead, he encouraged her to doubt that God meant what He said. Once he had positioned her on the slippery slope of doubt, he knew she would fall.

2. *He encourages people to make their own decisions about right and wrong.* Satan lured Eve into eating the fruit by telling her she would be like God if she did. God had given the first two people great knowledge and power over the materials of the world. What He did not give them was the ability to discern right from wrong; that he told them directly.

The power to make one's own decisions about morality is what Satan offered, knowing that when they possessed it, he could lead them astray. The enemy always wins when believers attempt to make moral judgments for themselves because they cannot avoid using the enemy's criteria. When the values come from self or society, they do not come from God.

Moral independence is one of Satan's most powerful temptations. Satan knows that people are weakest when it comes to themselves. He lured Eve with the promise of material benefit and increased knowledge, two devices that promote selfish interests. He uses these same two powerful weapons today to promote a self-centered, independent attitude.

In the United States during these last days, the enemy promotes the sin of self-centeredness as never before. At other times, in other places, societies have worshipped other gods. People make great personal sacrifice to these false gods. Yet in America, where people know the true God, they sacrifice nothing. They trust themselves, their possessions, and their knowledge.

Jesus teaches that denying this independence is the fundamental task of the Christian life. *"If anyone would come after me, he must deny himself and take up his cross daily and follow me"* (Luke 9:23). Paul refers to this as the problem of serving the "flesh" or the old sinful nature (see Romans 5-8). Each of us inherited an old nature from the fall of Adam and Eve that continually pushes for gratification of selfish desires. When self-centeredness wins out in a person's life, Satan has won a battle over that person.

3. Satan uses persecution to bodily harm God's children; he uses deception to spiritually harm them. Satan victimizes Christians through their own selfish desires by encouraging them to address only personal wants. Serving oneself can cause great damage.

In verse 6, Satan reveals his primary deceptive devices. Eve thought the fruit would taste good, looked good, and that eating it would yield wisdom. *The lust of the flesh, the lust of the eye, and the pride of life.* The enemy used these three selfish desires to ruin the life Adam and Eve had in Eden, and he uses them today, through the power and great influence of the beast-system, to lead Christians from the joyful life they have in Christ, to the lonely place of self-gratification and self-preservation.

Satan used each of these strategies to tempt Christ. First, he tried the lust of the flesh. After 40 days without food, Jesus was famished. When Satan appeared, he did not challenge Jesus' relationship to His Father. He did not try to get Jesus to believe that God had abandoned him, or that God did not love him because he demanded such sacrifice. Instead, he played to Jesus' sense of self. *"If you are the Son of God,"* Satan challenged, *"tell these stones to become bread."* Jesus responded with the ultimate retort, *"It is written: 'Man does not live on bread alone, but on every word that comes from the mouth of God'"* (Matthew 4:3-4).

Next, Satan tried the pride of life. As they stood on the highest point of the temple, Satan quoted Scripture.

"If you are the son of God," he said, "throw yourself down. For it is written:" 'He will command his angels concerning you, and they will lift you up in their hands, so that you will not strike your foot against a stone.' " (Matthew 4:6)

If Satan had had his way, Jesus would have shown great pride in being God's son by doing a foolish act simply to invoke divine intervention. But Jesus responded by quoting Scripture.

Finally, Satan used the lust of the eyes. From a high place, he showed Jesus all the world at his feet, telling Jesus he could have all he could see. Jesus was offered all the things of the world and He refused. How little Satan offers God's children, and they accept.

4. Satan's most powerful form of deception makes reference to God. He gets God's people to serve their own interests by invoking God's interests. Many times Satan does not tempt Christians with things they believe to be evil. He's too clever for that. What he does is to get believers to follow him by using God's name. When Christians rely on worldly means to achieve spiritual ends, Satan has accomplished this trick.

Summarizing Revelation 13:7a

Satan knows that man's greatest weakness is "serving self." As Paul states in Romans 7, it is a law, a part of man's nature. As Satan observes the strength of God's people in any area, he strikes out against God by maneuvering his worldly systems to attack. This attack may be direct and obvious through *persecution* or he may use *deception.* Through Satan's use of deception, he creates an overpowering temptation to serve the flesh or self—such as a lust for material things and the use of man's reasoning to determine right and wrong. It is prophesied that near the end of time there will be a society functioning under the beast-system that will gain the throne of the world and be stronger in its worldly influences than any previous society. The influence of our present day media, which never existed before the last 50 years or so, is an example. Ninety-five percent of it is controlled by our spiritual enemy, Satan.

The Apostle Paul teaches that it is a part of our old nature to have selfish wants, but not to the extent we now find in our society. Not to the extent where so many serve "self" like a god. This contrast can be seen by studying societies in other countries. They also are born with natural desires. They also are related to Adam, but they don't serve "self" like a god. In many countries the people serve a false god, yet we find them making great sacrifices to these gods. A man's true god is that for which he serves and sacrifices the most.

Satan's objective in a society of strong Christian influence is to develop a worldly influence so strong that those who think they are serving Christianity will make "self" their god. He tempts them to develop an attitude of "independence" just as he tempted Adam and Eve and others of God's people down through the ages. The Word of God confirms this is the basic character of Satan. Speaking of Satan, Isaiah stated, *"You said in your heart, 'I will ascend to heaven; I will raise my throne above the stars of God; I will sit enthroned on the mount of assembly, on the utmost heights of the sacred mountain. I will ascend above the tops of the clouds; I will make myself like the Most High'"* (Isaiah 14:13-14). The use of the pronoun "I" (promoting self) describes Satan's character. It is the expression of an "independent attitude."

These words, spoken through Isaiah by the Holy Spirit about Satan, teach us that the spirit of Satan is characterized by: (1) "self"-assertion, (2) "self"-satisfaction, (3) "self"-exaltation, and (4) "self"-glorification. These four personal characteristics are attributed to the being of Satan. It is important to realize that the degree to which we are controlled by the spirit of Satan does not have to be expressed by some kind of satanic worship. It can be, and usually is, expressed by the degree to which we worship and serve "self."

Satan's enemy is God. Therefore, his most enticing and least detectable attacks will be against God's children in the geographical area where Christianity is strongest. Satan is no dummy; he attacks where it will hurt God the most. We learn this from Adam and Eve, Israel, Jesus, and the early church. And in our earlier review of Matthew 4:1-10, we discovered that Satan did not tempt Jesus with the obvious vices of the world. He didn't even tempt Him to deny God or to quit being religious. He tempted Jesus with self-serving attractions to step out on His own, to become independent and make his own decisions.

In Revelation 13:7 John states: *"He (the beast-superpower) was given power to make war against the saints and to conquer them."* The beast-system has been given power to make spiritual war against the saints and has overcome many, causing them to fall away from following true biblical Christian standards. This is another prophecy, given by John about the end-time-beast-superpower, which we are seeing fulfilled before our eyes.

CHAPTER SEVEN

REVELATION 13:7b-8

And he (the beast-superpower) was given authority over every tribe, people, language and nation. All inhabitants of the earth will worship the beast—all whose names have not been written in the book of life belonging to the Lamb that was slain from the creation of the world.

John foretells of the beast's—ultimately Satan's—fearsome power over both the people of God and the people of the world. And he says that *"every tribe, people, language and nation"* will fall under the superpower's control, and that *"all the inhabitants of the earth"* will worship the superpower. To comprehend how the United States fits into this requires a closer look at these key phrases.

Throughout Scripture prophets often foretell of a condition or general state of affairs, even though the actual fulfillment of a happening may not occur. Daniel, for example, wrote of empires that controlled the world, yet Babylon, Persia, Greece, and Rome controlled only a limited part of the earth's topography. They influenced the mainstream of civilization as will be the case with any superpower. Daniel is illustrating the power of these empires and their worldly influence over all peoples.

Every Tribe, People, Language and Nation

For John to write that the end-time superpower will exercise authority over *"every tribe, people, language, and nation"* does not disqualify the United States. Clearly, the United States Government does not directly control every person on the globe. Yet the United States does influence, in a general sense, nations and peoples throughout the world through the authority of its leadership in world politics, economics, military, and industrial power. The inhabitants of remote places receive American products and American visitors. Those who do not speak English learn about American culture through music and electronic communication. Countries without formal political ties to the United States cannot escape United States foreign policy. The United States is like a giant surrounded by tiny people; whether the giant walks, stands, sits, or lies down, others are affected.

All the Earth's Inhabitants

The phrase, *"all the inhabitants of the earth will worship the beast,"* is an expression of American power similar to *"every tribe, people, language and nation."*

To "worship," or to hold in awe, aptly describes the image of America in the minds of people throughout the world. They may admire the American standard of living, or resent American control of their governments and economies. But they respect and hold in awe American power and life-style which is a form of worship. Missionaries often confirm this point.

This covers our Bible study of the descriptive characteristics John gives that identify the end-time beast-superpower he prophesied about in Revelation 13. Verse 9 and 10 of this chapter state a biblical principle, and verses 11 through 18 discuss areas of concern about the influence of the society functioning under this beast-superpower which I will briefly review in chapters 9, 10, and 11. For even greater detail on this penetrating influence, see my other two books.

>-+-<>-+-0-+-<>-+-<

CHAPTER EIGHT

DANIEL AND THE END-TIME BEAST-SUPERPOWER

Before examining other verses in Revelation 13, it is useful to look more closely at Daniel's vision. In the Book of Daniel, the prophet Daniel describes a vision that contains some images common to John's vision. He writes of a *"beast,"* with *"ten horns,"* with a mouth that spoke *"boastfully."* Could two men who lived centuries apart be describing the same vision? The short answer is "yes" and "no." Both Daniel and John write of the last-days superpower, although each has a different reference point.

Daniel was among the first Jewish captives taken to Babylon in 606 BC by King Nebuchadnezzar. Daniel, a young man of God, remained true to his Jewish heritage during his years in captivity despite the influence of Babylonian culture around him. God honored his commitment to his faith and gave him learning abilities, including the interpretation of prophetic dreams.

When King Nebuchadnezzar was troubled by a dream, he commanded his wise men to reveal the content of the dream and its meaning. The court magicians could not, but Daniel could because God had given him a revelation (see Daniel 2). The king had dreamed, Daniel said, of a metallic man with feet of clay. Daniel explained that each of the component materials represented empires that would rule the earth. Nebuchadnezzar was so impressed by Daniel's abilities that he proclaimed the Jewish prophet governor of the province of Babylon and chief of the wise men. Daniel became a leading figure of the royal court (Daniel 2:48-49).

Later, Daniel began to receive his own prophetic dreams (Daniel 7:1). In these visions, God revealed the worldly empires from Daniel's day until the end of time that would have a strong effect on the people of Israel. Following the destruction of Jerusalem by Roman legions in 70 AD, the great Diaspora began, the dispersion of Jewish people throughout the world. The modern state of Israel began May 14, 1948, after the return of Jewish exiles to Palestine. Therefore, Daniel does not prophesy about empires between 70 AD and 1948, because Israel did not exist as a nation during that time. Therefore, his prophecy would be of that beast, that empire before 70 AD, and the origin of that end-time world power that has a great amount of influence on Israel after it became a nation in 1948. It is essential to understand that Daniel's prophecies were centered around his people, their nation, and those superpowers that helped shape Israel's history.

Daniel 7:7-8

> *After that, in my vision at night I looked, and there before me was a fourth beast—terrifying and frightening and very powerful. It had large iron teeth; it crushed and devoured its victims and trampled under foot whatever was left. It was different from all the former beasts, and it had ten horns. While I was thinking about the horns, there before me was another horn, a little one, which came up among them; and three of the first horns were uprooted before it. This horn had eyes like the eyes of a man and a mouth that spoke boastfully.*

In these two verses Daniel describes a ten-horned beast that is similar to the beast John describes. Daniel, however, is not describing the same beast as John.

Daniel wanted to know the identity of this fourth beast, the unnamed beast with iron teeth. He wanted to know about the ten horns, and the horn that came up, before which three horns fell (Daniel 7:19-20). In the verses that follow, Daniel receives his answers.

Daniel 7:23-25

The fourth beast is a fourth kingdom that will appear on earth. It will be different from all the other kingdoms and will devour the whole earth, trampling it down and crushing it. The ten horns are ten kings who will come from this kingdom. After them another king will arise, different from the earlier ones; he will subdue three kings. He will speak against the Most High and oppress his saints and try to change the set times and the laws. The saints will be handed over to him for a time, times and half a time.

These verses unlock the symbolic meaning of several of the words and phrases used in verses 20 and 21. Other words used in verses 23 through 25 may be understood from my earlier discussion. History and Bible scholars agree that the "fourth beast" refers to the Roman Empire. "Horn" and "king" refer to nations with substantial power and influence. "Little horn" would mean a young, or new nation. The little horn grew out of the ten horns and remained *distinct* or separate. This is the meaning of the Hebrew word translated as *"among"* in verse 8.

Daniel prophesied of those world empires in existence from his time until the end of time that greatly influenced Israel as a nation. The little horn or nation he introduces in chapter 7, which arises out of the countries from the Roman Empire, will be that superpower influencing Israel after she regains her position as a nation near the end of time. The United States is a young, new nation and has been the ruling influential power over Israel since the historical event took place in 1948.

Daniel's Prophecy

Putting these interpretations together reveals a prophecy that unfolds like this:

1. Out of the Roman Empire emerges a bloc of prominent countries.

2. Out of this bloc comes a new country comprised of people from the Roman Empire.

3. This new country defeats three of the other countries in order to achieve its separate status.

4. This new country gains power and influence to an extent greater than any of the countries from which its people came.

5. After reaching the status of a power with worldwide influence, this new country turns on the saints. The nation wears down the saints to the point of overwhelming them.

6. The Christians are worn down or defeated for a period of time—*"a time, times and a half time."* During this period, the nation changes its laws to control the people within the land.

These six events describe the American situation quite well. Daniel explains how Europe emerges from its position as the northern region of Rome's empire, and how the United States came together from the peoples of Europe. He tells how the United States had to defeat three nations, which is what happened—England, France, and Spain—for control of its territory in North America. He also tells how the United States went on to become a superpower, which was after World War II, then turns against its Christian members by changing many of the laws of its society. He tells how Christians become overwhelmed, and of their government which contributes to their ineffectual state.

No other country even comes close to fulfilling these prophesies. A nation, barely 200 years old, becomes a superpower. It becomes the mightiest empire in world history, and as a worldwide empire, it has had a unique influence over both the Jewish people as prophesied by Daniel, and Christians as prophesied by John in Revelation 13. John and Daniel both prophesied of this last government superpower, and their approach is similar, but with different points of reference.

Revived Roman Empire

The beast that John prophesies about in Revelation 13:1 is without a doubt the ancient Roman Empire reappearing upon the world scene. Many historians and scholars have described a resemblance of the old Roman Empire and contemporary American society. The two societies share common things, such as government, commerce, militarism, and an emphasis on hedonistic things, such as food, pleasure, athletics, building, and deterioration of moral standards. So similar are the two that a recent President commissioned a study to learn why Rome collapsed so that America might avoid the same collapse.

It is interesting to note that many of the first to settle North America trace their ancestors to the ancient Roman Empire. Rome controlled central Europe along with Britain, and many of the first immigrants were of German, Dutch, French, and English stock. John indicates that Rome's reappearance will display a particular characteristic. In Revelation 12:17 (RSV), John saw Satan standing *"on the sand of the sea."* The United States revived the Roman Empire across the Atlantic ocean.

The revived Roman Empire bears a similarity to the fulfillment of a prophecy during the time of Jesus. When Jesus walked the earth, Jewish scholars anticipated the reappearance of the prophet Elijah according to Old Testament prophecy that the prophet would precede the coming of the Messiah. Scripture says that this prophecy was fulfilled by John the Baptist (Matthew 11:14, Luke 1:17). John the Baptist fulfilled the prophecy because his personality and character, or spirit, were like that of Elijah's. In this same way the United States fulfills the prophesied reappearance of the Roman Empire. The same spirit that prevailed in pagan Rome characterizes contemporary American society. And just as religious leaders in Jesus' day did not recognize the fulfillment of prophesy concerning Elijah, so many Christians today do not realize the fulfillment of prophecy concerning ancient Rome.

►┼◄►─O─◄┼◄

CHAPTER NINE

REVELATION 13:11

*Then I saw another beast, coming out of the earth.
He had two horns like a lamb, but he spoke like a
dragon.*

The Second Beast

The first beast arose *"out of the sea"* (Revelation 13:1). It is the
United States Government which assumed the throne of Satan's
kingdom at the end of World War II. The second beast that John
now prophesies about arose *"out of the earth."* It is subject to, and
serves the interest of, the first beast. This second beast symbolizes
the power of American society, specifically, the teaching influence
through modern technology and values that develop after the first
beast gains the throne of the world. Its influence is so powerful,
so dynamic, that John also makes reference to it as a beast. This
second beast appears harmless *("like a lamb")* but represents the per-
verted values that accompany the first beast's ascendancy to power
("spoke like a dragon"); values alien to what they should be in a normal society (Daniel 7:25). Reading John's prophetic words, this
second beast has the appearance of a false prophet, proclaiming
godly interest while teaching false values about spiritual matters
and standards.

The Unholy War

Christians who have kept their heads out of the sand these past few decades realize the frightful moral deterioration of America. We are, it cannot be denied, engaged in a revolutionary war. This revolution is a cultural war fought over the hearts and minds of the American people and their life-style.

Since the close of World War II, American traditional values have turned topsy-turvy in almost every area. Thirty million babies have been slaughtered through the "free choice" of abortion. Homosexuality, regarded only a few years ago as a criminal act, has now become an "alternative life-style." Pornography regularly appears on television, in movies, books, and magazines. The family, under attack from all sides, disintegrates as school children from kindergarten to high school are taught how to enjoy "safe sex" and "alternative life-styles." The government toys with murderers, rapists, and robbers by often giving them light or negligible prison sentences while it criminalizes the moral activities of Christians. Christian leaders, organizations, and individuals find themselves the target of vicious verbal persecution by government, media and cultural elites who more and more reject our traditional biblical foundation. Those who stand against the destruction of human life can now be prosecuted under statutes designed to combat organized crime, while newly-enacted asset forfeiture laws are used to seize the property of honest, law-abiding citizens.

Television and print media often portray those who fear God as unbalanced extremists and are beginning to equate fundamental Christians with "dangerous cults" and "dangerous cult members." As people: *who* frequently attend church and Bible studies; *who* believe in the second coming of Christ; *who* give a lot to their churches; *who* are anti-gay and anti-abortion; *who* separate themselves from mainstream society; and *who* "practice child abuse by following a strict disciplinary code and use Bible verses like '*spare the rod and spoil the child*' to justify physical discipline" (*New York Times* March 7, 1993).

Our government occupies a central place in this unholy war against the saints. Each year, tens of thousands of regulations appear, designed to control every aspect of American lives. Each

United States citizen is responsible to know, understand, and follow every one of these new laws and regulations. In 1992 alone, the Federal Government filled the *Federal Register* with 67,715 pages of finely-printed regulations. The volume of law books filled by government each year are turned over to several dozen applicable Federal agencies, that, with the labor of 121,000 people they employ, write thousands of new regulations to implement and enforce these new laws.

The Clean Water Act, Clean Air Act, and a host of other environmental laws passed in recent years, represent just one of the dictatorial controls the government has claimed for itself. They want Americans to believe these measures protect the nation's natural resources, but the hidden agenda is governmental control. Not trees, not water, not wildlife, but control over every business, every privately-held property, every automobile, and every action of every person in America. The real agenda is more government control, not environmentalism. The truth is, there is really very little truth presented by the government and the media.

The original principles of this society, established at the nation's founding and preserved with patriot's blood, now face a great attack. I can barely suggest the broad outlines of this attack in the few pages I have here, the attack comes with such hideous strength. The call for the naturalization of children, the abolition of the family, the promotion of promiscuity, the obliteration of private life and the installation of Orwellian controls over every aspect of life, is the administration's agenda and now to be accelerated in what can only be called the greatest onslaught against American Christianity since the birth of the nation.

The Mind Behind the System

Has this cultural war, this uprooting within a single generation of America's traditional way of life, happened on its own? Have values slipped by accident? Morality spontaneously decayed? No, it has not! John identifies the spiritual force behind the corruption of America. This second beast orchestrates the transformation of this nation for a purpose, by means of a strategy intended to destroy the will of those who would resist. The strategy is to permanently alter the way in which people think about social problems and individual actions. Good is bad, bad people good, in a cultural transformation so complete that Americans will lack the ability to identify the source of their oppression.

Satan utilizes the material world, the people of the world, and the value systems of the world. He has raised up in our society a society that exalts itself far above all the other societies of the world. American society has perfected all of the characteristics of his world system, and consequently, possesses great power to tempt Christians to step outside of God's Word.

No longer is it necessary to go out into the world in order to make contact with it. Through the electronic media the influences of our society now come and search us out, they captivate people daily. As never before, the Christian family today feels the pull of a worldly society and its ways. Our apathy toward crime, sexual permissiveness, and world problems has revealed that we are willing to let Satan do anything in the world just so long as it doesn't affect our personal well being. The result is that many Christians now place a greater emphasis on supplying the physical needs and wants of their families than in supplying the spiritual needs.

Satan is using the philosophy of our society to deceive and paralyze God's people in many areas of Christian teaching. It is a society Satan has used to influence both Christians and non-Christians to become overly concerned about serving themselves. Many Christians have set themselves above the cause of Christ by their preoccupation with their own wants and concerns. Too many of us are preoccupied with serving self: "my well being," "my pleasures," "my desires," "my ambitions," "things being done my way."

The result is that Christian values which shaped people's lives for centuries in our nation have eroded in a generation since our country became the greatest superpower on the face of the earth after World War II. The unthinkable has now become acceptable. The evidence reflects that a majority of our population has simply lost the ability to discern between right and wrong.

Since America gained the throne of the world, it has become a very sinful nation. Our cup of iniquity has been overfilled with senseless violence, crime, the murder of millions of babies through abortion, corruption, rampant divorce, adultery, pornography, and child molestation. Homosexuality is flaunted as a legitimate lifestyle. Drunkenness and drug abuse is at epidemic proportions; as a nation, Americans now spend more dollars on illegal drugs than we spend on food, clothing, and shelter combined. Our main source of entertainment, the movie theater and television, is filled with violence, sex, and greed.

We in the church often present the concept of the beast in the book of Revelation to mean some kind of monstrosity. One of the oldest literary devices is to make good things beautiful and evil things ugly. In the stories and legends we learned as children, bad things are represented by monsters, hags, and subhuman figures, while good things are presented by handsome young men and fair maidens. Artists use a scaly, horned figure with a tail to depict the Devil himself, yet the Scripture reveals that he appears *"as an angel of light"* (2 Corinthians 11:14). As John prophetically describes in Revelation 13:11, the teaching power (two horns) of our society (beast out of the earth), may appear harmless (like a lamb) but the spirit of the philosophy being taught (spoke like a dragon) in our culture since the first beast came to power has been an overwhelming influence to develop the anti-Christ characteristics centered in "serving self." The very character and teaching of Satan. (See II Timothy 3:1-5 and Isaiah 14:12-14.)

>-+-<>-+-O-+-<>-+-<

CHAPTER TEN

REVELATION 13:12-16

He (the second beast) exercised all the authority of the first beast on his behalf, and made the earth and its inhabitants worship the first beast, whose fatal wound had been healed. And he performed great and miraculous signs, even causing fire to come down from heaven to earth in full view of men. Because of the signs he was given power to do on behalf of the first beast, he deceived the inhabitants of the earth. He ordered them to set up an image in honor of the beast who was wounded by the sword and yet lived. He was given power to give breath to the image of the first beast, so that it could speak and cause all who refused to worship the image to be killed.

In the past, great empires or superpowers have relied on military might and political clout to dominate and control other countries. They would plunder the goods of the people and often place heavy taxes on them. Even in modern times, communism, for example, ruled through the "barrel of a gun." But the beast-superpower of Revelation 13 uses a uniquely different method of power to help influence and dominate other peoples. It has been through the technological power of its society (the second beast which came up out of the earth) to produce and supply other nations their goods and services.

Electronic Technology's Role

Since World War II, our society's tremendous advancement to world leadership has primarily been the outgrowth of our electronic technology. Most of these developments we take for granted and consider commonplace, but John accurately describes them as the performance of *"great and miraculous signs, even causing fire to come down from heaven to earth in full view of men"*—space shots, etc., done *"on behalf of the first beast"*—our government.

I am not saying that there is something inherently bad about electricity or electronic technology. As a part of God's creation, electric power can be used for many wonderful things. But Satan controls the world, and the things electricity makes possible are therefore part of his worldly system. Electronic media, primarily television, provides a subtle, yet devastating power source. Television provides a direct means of mind control, a powerful means of influence that appears harmless.

Do you recognize the false prophet of television? It is a false prophet. Anything that has the ability to plant thoughts in our minds is a teacher, a potential deceiver. These days, it is not difficult to spot television programs filled with sex and violence that are clearly evil. But the endless array of "harmless" programs—the "decent" movies, game shows, and commercials can also be powerful tools of Satan because they promote the anti-Christ message of "self-centeredness." Television offers "entertainment," which seems harmless enough, but deceives because it overdevelops the sense of "serving self." Personal sacrifice, delayed gratification, thinking of and giving to others first are themes usually alien to television.

The creation of electronic media in the twentieth century has allowed Satan to capture human imagination as never before in human history. The expansion of network and cable television in recent years has provided Satan with a medium of teaching influence for every minute of every hour of every day.

A curious invention of the 1920s, TV rapidly became part of American households after World War II. Before the '50s, television stopped broadcasting at ten o'clock in the evening. But in 1950, late-night television began to appear. Since then, the idea that there should be a time and space reserved for family life has vanished. Today, the stream of films, programs, and commercials pour into American households around the clock.

It is impossible to overstate the impact of video on modern society. Did you know that the United States leads the world in the production of TV programming? The American film and television industries have no significant foreign competitors. Total U.S. television exports are estimated to be about 150,000 hours; 50,000 sent to Latin America, 50,000 to Asia, and 50,000 to Europe. U.S. programs are watched by viewers in faraway places around the world.

The United States exports its immoral life-style across the globe; we influence the people of other nations adversely. The influence of American cinema has never been greater. America's perverse values—through the second beast—exercise power of influence beyond imagination.

An Image

In these verses, John explains how the spiritual influence of our society will make people fashion an "image" for the first beast. The Greek word used for image is *eikon*, a word that means "representation" and "manifestation." It is a representation or manifestation of the first beast which is crafted by the second, and is used, John says in verse 17, *"so that no one could buy or sell unless he had the mark."* John's prophetic language here is not so incomprehensible as it may appear. John says, in other words, that the technology of American society (the second beast) develops the ability for the United States Government (the first beast) through some means (the image) by which the government (the first beast) will control (by use of the mark) the commercial activities (buying and selling) of its citizens.

What is this image? Consistent with the description given by John's prophecy, I believe it refers to a development out of modern-day technology, more specifically, the electronic computer. No other machine in human history matches the influence of the computer. Since World War II, when the first beast began to reign over Satan's kingdom—the world—this amazing machine has become part of every facet of public and private life. Computers perform such an astonishing array of activities that modern life, as we live it today, would be impossible without them. They possess a powerful technological brain, the microchip.

The entire world of commerce and industry now functions by use of computers. Transportation, from interstate trucking to airlines, relies on computers for everything from navigation to the scheduling of maintenance. Medicine, from diagnosing illness to filling prescriptions to cure them, relies on computers. Department stores, banks, hospitals, utilities, post offices, universities, every modern institution, functions by means of computer technology.

American confidence in computer technology has often replaced faith in God. Technology has become the theology of our system that promises salvation by materialism. The pursuit of more and better things, made possible by the tiny computer chip, has replaced the ethic of hard work and clean living within the American character. When trouble comes, Americans—American Christians included—will often turn more to technology for help rather than renew their faith in Christ. What more apt recreation of modern life than the human creation that makes it possible, this far-reaching technological achievement, the electronic computer. It is truly an image, or representation and manifestation of modern-day technology that fulfills all of John's prophecy.

I do not understand all that John prophesies about in these verses. Yet the harnessing of the earth's electromagnetic force, which appeared solely as lightning in the sky just a few hundred years ago, and its use in a device capable of performing complex human activities including reproduction of the human voice, fits John's references to the second beast's ability to make *fire to come down from heaven to earth*" and "*give breath to the image of the first beast, so that it could speak.*" Several years ago *Time Magazine*, January 3, 1983, announced its man of the year for 1982 is not a man, but the computer.

It appears from John's statement, *"cause all who refused to worship the image to be killed,"* that those who remain loyal to Christ and refuse to be controlled by a computer system in the future, could face prison or death. Man in his great wisdom may decide to actually put to death those who refuse to go along. Man's wisdom has always been foolishness with God and will be used for his own destruction. It tends to be anti-Christ for it makes us depend on ourselves and the things of this world, rather than Christ.

►─◄►─०─◄►─◄

CHAPTER ELEVEN

REVELATION 13:16-18

He (the beast) also forced everyone, small and great, rich and poor, free and slave, to receive a mark on his right hand or on his forehead, so that no one could buy or sell unless he had the mark, which is the name of the beast or the number of his name. This calls for wisdom. If anyone has insight, let him calculate the number of the beast, for it is man's number. His number is 666.

In Revelation 13:16-18, John points to the day when the beast— the United States Government—will control economic transactions. It is difficult to say what these commercial regulations will entail, but some kind of marking system will be imposed. John says that *"no one could buy or sell unless he had the mark,"* which ties the marking system to the beast's system for economic control. Exactly what form this economic control will take cannot be answered with absolute certainty. However, a marking system of the kind John describes has already been developed.

The Mark of the Beast

Did you know that "666" can be found on practically every item on grocery and retail store shelves? The UPC symbol technology has been in place in the United States since 1973. As the *Los Angeles Times* explained it:

The grocery store industry has developed what it calls the Universal Product Code (UPC), which to the consumer looks like a series of vertical lines covering an area about the size of a large postage stamp.[1]

The purpose of the UPC bar code is to standardize product identification for use with automated cash register equipment. What is of interest from the perspective of Bible prophecy is that every UPC code contains three unidentified marks corresponding to the number 666. Students of Bible prophecy know that sixes are among the secrets of the economy destined to close out this, the Gentile Age. These three sixes are the key working numbers for every version of the UPC code. Computer experts I have consulted have told me that the triple-six pattern has become a universal design standard; it cannot be changed.

Most Common UPC Design

Most of the marks, or bars, in the symbol are identified by numbers at the bottom of the code. But there are always at least three unidentified bars. In this design, these marks appear on the far left, in the middle, and at the far right. Three of these unidentified marks are always the number 6. You can compare some of the bar codes found on products in your own home with the *interpretation standard* for bar code design. You will discover three unidentified marks on any code you inspect. These marks always translate into three sixes.

Interpretation Standard for Bar Codes

Set #1 is designated by the number 1
Set #2 is designated by the number 2
Set #3 is designated by the number 3

Why is the number six used in this way? Computer techni-
cians say that 6 is the perfect computer number. Six is the perfect
number because computers work on a series of six cores that allow
current to change direction in order to perform switching operations.
The formula for this system is 6 60 6. The six cores work in con-
junction with 60 displacements × 6 (one character—one bit of
information). To number a card, person, or item, the transaction
must be prefixed *six hundred, threescore, and six,* just as John said in
Revelation 13:18. Apple Computer Inc. celebrated the number 6
as the perfect computer number when it introduced the first 200
Apple I's to be retailed for $666.66.[2]

Although the bar codes on grocery items are the most notice-
able, credit and bank cards make use of bar codes, too. These are
micro-encoded along the magnetic strip on the back of the card.
When these marks are scanned by laser light, the optical pattern is
converted to an electrical signal (analog), which is converted in turn
to a digital signal, then decoded by a microprocessor. Literally tens
of thousands of characters can be micro-encoded on the three by
one half inch magnetic strip on a single card. A little more auto-
mation is all it would take to generate a personal record of every
person's purchases, transactions, and so on.

New Economic Era

When will the beast's system of economic control unfold?
Again, this cannot be answered precisely. The technology for a cashless society already exists. Credit cards make the introduction of a
national identification card possible right now. In addition, existing
laser technology could be used to implant information beneath the
skin on the head, arm, or some other place on the body. The
manipulation of such technology for social control might follow a
major social or political event, appear in the aftermath of a
natural disaster, or result from the fallout of a major economic
shake-up.

The condition of our economic system is very important in light
of Christians living in the beast system. Do you remember the stock
market crash of October 19, 1987? It seems to have come and gone
without serious fallout. At the time, however, many people
expressed great concern because the crash sent a clear message of

the extreme financial and economic vulnerability that exists. No matter what triggered this Black Monday, if our financial markets were sound, a plunge of this speed and magnitude could not have happened.

The crash was merely one of several indications that something is terribly wrong with our economy. It was a warning! The failure of the savings and loan system is another. There is an underlying structural problem, a problem that appears to be irreversible. Let us look at this problem and what caused it to develop.

From Prosperity to Heavy Debt

To understand our current financial troubles, it's necessary to go back to the 1940s. World War II left the nations of Europe and the Pacific Rim in shambles. Many people lost their homes, and they lost their means of livelihood as well. The fighting destroyed factories, businesses, power plants, roads, bridges, rail lines, and more. Germany, England, Japan, and many other nations lost their industrial capacity. The infrastructure needed for economic productivity had been wiped out. At the same time, these nations lost a whole generation of industrial and government managers. The leadership necessary for business enterprise took a serious blow. Consequently, the economic strength of these nations experienced a severe economic setback. England, for example, has never really recovered. Rationing of food, oil, and other staple commodities continued for years after the war. It went from an industrial power with globe-encircling interests to a declining nation with a modest role in international affairs.

But while the European and Pacific powers crawled out from under the rubble, the United States was well on its way to economic supremacy. World War II enhanced America's fortunes. None of the fighting had occurred on American soil, so the United States emerged as the only major power with its industrial and agricultural bases intact. Wartime production pulled the domestic economy out of the Depression, and a wide sector of the economy never demobilized. United States workers made huge economic gains. Few of those in the industrial world could boast higher pay, more extensive fringe benefits, or better working conditions. Production within American factories continued at a steady clip as the United

States was in a unique position to furnish its wartime allies and enemies with many of the products and services their people needed. During the next 30 years, American products achieved a world-wide reputation. It was the "great society" emerging—the beast which came out of the earth—while the first beast watched.

The postwar years gave American companies a tremendous head start. The lack of foreign competition combined with Yankee know-how catapulted the United States to leadership in many economic sectors. The United States captured first place in the production of automobiles, machine tools, electronic equipment, and other vital industries. American factories became models of industrial excellence as American technology and management expertise set the standard. Not surprisingly, few Americans wanted to buy foreign products. American consumers refused foreign imports, which they bad-mouthed as shoddy imitations. We preferred high quality domestic products to second rate goods manufactured abroad. This created an impressive trade surplus. Year after year, Americans sold far more than they bought, and billions of excess dollars poured into the United States economy. We provided the major share of the goods and services needed around the world.

As a result, the American standard of living shot up beyond imagination. Americans claimed vast worldly possessions unprecedented in world history. With less than 7 percent of the world's population, we accumulated half of the world's wealth and consumed a full third of the world's resources each year. American factories churned out top quality products, and thick-walleted American consumers snapped them up. Americans, because they earned high wages, could purchase the steady flow of products from domestic factories. This availability of consumer goods allowed Americans to live better than virtually every other people throughout the world. Those categorized as "poor" in America would have made the "upper class" in many countries. The American life style became the envy of the world as Americans routinely enjoyed products and services completely out of reach for people in other lands.

But then, the tide began to turn. The military obligations the United States had incurred around the globe following the war meant massive government spending. The American economy became dependent on foreign oil, and the oil producing nations

organized to charge more. American industries lost their technological edge. More important, the rest of the world regained its
industrial capacity. European and Asian competitors caught up and
began to pass us within industries pioneered in the United States.
They had developed efficient production methods and rigid quality
control standards. Imported clothing, Asian electronic goods, and
foreign cars meant value for the American consumer. And for the
first time in nearly half a century, Americans began buying more
foreign goods than they were selling. Rather than a healthy trade
surplus, we generated a massive trade deficit.

Now we find ourselves in a difficult financial situation. We
should scale down our standard of living to meet our diminished
economic position in the world, but we are not doing so. In fact,
Americans expectations have *increased*, not decreased. Using the
generation born after the war as a benchmark, Americans have got-
ten used to the idea of living with more, even though we already
enjoy a standard of living unknown before. For some, it's a matter
of greed. They already have more than people almost everywhere
in the world, but still they are not satisfied. But for most Americans, I believe it's a matter of ignoring economic reality. Most of
us have grown accustomed to the material possessions that make
up what we call "the good life." Few seem to realize that they are
victims of a worldly deception that ensnares people through
irresistible advertising and product availability. We claim as our
birthright a standard of living that took a world war to bring about.
We have been led to expect a life style that is getting harder and
harder to achieve.

Since the 1970s, the widening gap between expectations and
capabilities has created an irreversible dependence on credit. Without the billions of dollars exports pump into the economy, the only
way for us to finance our living standard is to borrow. Buying on
credit is the only way for many Americans to get what they need—
or are enticed by the world-system to want. Few understand the
reality of this nation's economic position vis-a-vis the rest of the
world. We have fallen into heavy debt. Personal debt has reached
a record high, savings an all-time low. Government is in the same
boat. Cities, states, and the Federal Government must
borrow in order to maintain the public services people have grown

accustomed to. Credit has put a stranglehold on our economy. The ability to borrow drives consumer spending, business expansion, and government services. As a consequence, the United States is in debt, serious debt.

The Economic Black Hole

In America, economic reality means indebtedness. It would be convenient to ignore this, but the consequences of our nation's reversal of fortune since the 1940s is inescapable. During the 1980s, our country shifted from being the largest creditor nation in the world to being the largest debtor nation. People face huge personal debt. Corporations juggle massive business debt. Government operates with huge deficits.

By supplying the rest of the world with many of its goods and services after World War II, Americans were able to enjoy a standard of living that was unheard of before. We have artificially maintained this living standard in recent years through credit. The insurmountable debt that has resulted casts a gloomy shadow over America's economic future.

Few politicians and corporate chieftains seem willing to admit there is a problem. Government officials and business leaders carry on as if nothing is wrong. In the rosy forecasts given by vested interest groups, the United States economy will rebound. In reality, it's more vulnerable to complete collapse than ever before. The years of unconscious overspending cannot be eradicated. No matter what the politicians promise, record indebtedness will ultimately result in financial judgment.

In a larger sense, what the government does or doesn't do at this point won't make much difference. Current "solutions" to the debt crisis amount to economic fiction rather than sound economic thinking. Take the idea of consumer spending. The notion is that the economy will be healthy as long as consumer spending remains strong. In other words, everybody will be poorer unless people spend more than they can afford. Does that make sense to you?

We will not be able to spend our way out of this crisis—that's the bottom line. Whether consumers spend more, or spend less; whether the government taxes more, or taxes less, the debt will con-tinue to grow. Traditional methods taken to prop up the economy simply are not feasible. No conventional solutions are available because this is an unheard of economic problem. Exactly how bad is the debt problem?

Federal Government Debt

Consider the federal deficit first. We have had enormous federal budget deficits since 1980. United States Government debt more than tripled from $800 billion at the beginning of 1980 to over $3 trillion by the end of 1990. Do you know what that means? It means the national government racked up over twice as much debt in a single decade—the 1980s—than it had accumulated during the previous 200 years of our country's history. The interest alone on that debt amounts to a full third of the annual budget.

Foreign Debt

Foreign debt is also staggering. Foreign debt—that's the amount the United States owes to other countries—jumped to $400 billion between 1979 and 1990. Who loans us this money? Our former enemy Japan is a significant source. It's ironic that our way of life now depends on the willingness of the Japanese to help finance it.

Consumer Debt

Now consider a kind of indebtedness that's closer to home. Since 1982, United States economic growth has been fueled by consumer debt. We, the consumers, have gone on an unprecedented spending spree. Outstanding consumer debt was $296 billion in 1982. At the end of 1990, it reached $800 billion. In economic terms, the American consumer is dangerously exposed with very little cash equity. The "spirit of merchandising" has grabbed people's hearts and caused staggering debt. Many American families depend on two incomes to meet their debt obligations; the loss of one income even for a brief period would tilt them dangerously close to financial ruin.

Business Debt

In addition to government and personal debt, there's business debt. Business debt rose from $1.3 trillion in 1982 to nearly $8 trillion by 1990. It's the United States Government, specifically, the

Federal Reserve, that finances this debt. In recent years the Federal Reserve has increased the money supply, that is, the amount of money it prints, at the fastest pace since World War II. During one recent six-year period, Money Stock (MI) rose over 50 percent.

We have mortgaged the future to pay for the present. In accumulating such terrific debt, we have charted a course that leads from riches to rags. At the root of this economic vulnerability is our failure to live within our means. *Installment debt, mortgage debt, government debt, plus corporate debt and other private debt has risen in a vain effort to maintain our present standard of living.* Probably sooner than later, the American people will be forced to accept a dramatically different living standard.

The debt-ridden United States economy has reached the point of no return. Americans have dug themselves a financial hole so deep that they will never climb out. Sooner than later, the system will have reached that critical point where the rising debt collides with falling earnings. When the right portion of debt goes unpaid, the credit system that drives our economy will falter. It's hard to say when the straw that breaks the camel's back—the shock that will trigger a major collapse—will happen. What will happen when the living standard we have known for so long begins to evaporate, no one can predict precisely. But there could be significant social and political fallout to a major economic catastrophe.

A major financial panic might bring civil disorder, violence, and unimaginable chaos, not necessarily because Americans lack basic necessities, but because they have been denied the things they have come to expect as their birthright. It's not the same in our country as it was during the Great Depression. During the 1930s, the majority of people were accustomed to working hard for simple necessities. The generation that survived the Depression was glad to have enough to eat, something to wear, and a roof over their heads. But the self-centered, materialistic, technology-fed generation of the 1980s and 1990s will not be content with that.

But whether or not there are riots in the streets following the impending financial crisis, *fear* of lawlessness and disorder will create an unprecedented reliance on government. As this nation's economic stability unravels, Americans will increasingly look to the government to do something major. Few will resist government intervention; many will demand it, including use of the military if necessary. It will be easy for government leaders of the beast-system to promise social order in return for absolute compliance. The government will have great incentive to eliminate perceived threats to the economy by extending control over buying and selling. When the next economic shock provokes deep-seated fear, people will cry out to the government to save them.

It is difficult to say what these commercial regulations will entail, but Bible prophecy clearly points to the day when the beast (the United States Government) will control economic transactions. A marking system of some kind will be imposed. In Revelation 13:16, John prophesies of a time when *"no one could buy or sell unless he has the mark."* He tied the marking system with the numbering system of the beast society as the method used for control. As stated earlier, a computer reads "marks" not numbers. Only by the wisdom of God could John have known this.

In his Times Square Church Pulpit Series Titled *The Witness of the Spirit*, dated 12/27/93, David Wilkerson states:

In President Clinton's health plan there is a provision for a national health identification card—and, eventually, a state-of-the-art, tamper-proof numbering system. This probably means an implantation device in the head, arm or somewhere on the body. No one will receive health coverage without a number.

(Capsule implants — computer chips — injected beneath the surface of the skin, are already widely promoted as hidden identification tags for tracking valuable livestock — cats, dogs, cattle, etc.)

We are also headed for a cashless society—first by credit card, and later by a laser implantation beneath the skin. The European Community has already planned for this. We may be on the very brink of the mark of the beast! And if you don't have discernment, you'll become an accessory to a murderous government system that takes your tax dollars for abortion!

Tragically, some Christians are not going to recognize these anti-Christ setups! That is why you need the Holy Spirit witness everyday—on your job, at work, at school. You'll need to rightly judge politicians and leaders so you'll not suddenly be sucked into the anti-Christ system.

►-+-◄►--O--◄►-+-◄

CHAPTER TWELVE

LIVING IN THE BEAST

Realizing that we are living under the beast of Revelation 13 is a sobering thought. Should Christians flee the United States to escape the beast? Will American believers face outright persecution for their faith? Should Americans refuse credit cards and avoid banks? These thoughts raise significant issues about how Christians should respond in general, and how we as individual Christians should conduct our lives. In this chapter and the one that follows, I provide some answers to each of these questions.

Flee the United States?

If you are a believer, you should not be overwhelmed by learning that the United States Government is the beast. At base, it means that the society in which we live is under the control of Satan, and that should not come as a surprise. Other societies— every society—is under the control of Satan. It's been this way since Adam and Eve left the Garden of Eden.

According to I John 5:19... *"the whole world is under the control of the evil one."* This means that the structure of everyday life is controlled by a prevailing principle that is alien to God. It would, therefore, be an exercise in futility to attempt to escape from the beast's grasp. Not merely because the beast now exerts worldwide influence, but because the whole world is under Satan's control to begin with.

Simply put, the beast represents no different threat than society. Society is contrary to God, the beast is contrary to God. Society—the beast—remains Satan's medium for attacking God's children. Believers should not attempt to escape the beast's influence, but learn to live the successful Christian life within its dominion.

The believer must live in the world. From that, there can be no escape. But what, specifically, should be the Christian's relationship to the United States Government? The answer, I believe, is found in Romans where Paul instructs those Christians living under another beast-superpower, the Roman Empire.

In the first seven verses of Chapter 13, Paul explains the nature of a Christian's citizenship under an unchristian government. The Roman Government, like our own in this present generation, rejected God's laws. The Roman Government opposed believers, and promoted pagan beliefs. Yet Paul did not teach believers to be anarchists, or to revolt. He taught those who feared God to respect the institution of government. God had instituted human governments to promote peaceable society and restrain selfishness and greed. This principle of respect applies to all governments, even those opposed to God. *"Everyone must submit himself to the governing authorities,"* Paul writes, *"for there is no authority except that which God has established"* (Romans 13:1).

It is difficult to respect a government that performs its God-ordained mission so poorly. Since the United States Government gained its superpower status, it has allowed a spirit of lawlessness to prevail. American society has become a violent, lawless society. Americans lead the world in homicide, rape and gun-related crime rates, and the government seems powerless to control this violence. Too many of those living in the United States fear nothing. No longer does the fear of government exist because government has proven incapable of retribution. The United States Government is failing at its God-ordained responsibility to maintain order.

Nevertheless, Paul says that Christians must not contribute to disorder. *"He who rebels against the authority is rebelling against what God has instituted, and those who do so will bring judgment on themselves"* (Romans 13:2). Government, no matter how terrible, portends no bad news for those who fear God. Government is *"God's*

servant, an agent of wrath to bring punishment on the wrongdoer"
(Romans 13:4), and Christians must... *"submit to the authorities,
not only because of possible punishment but also because of conscience"*
(Romans 13:5).

Christians ought to live in a law abiding, respectful, and coop-
erative manner. The ideal Christian concept of citizenship is to be
a model subject of earthly authority. *"Give everyone what you owe
him: If you owe taxes, pay taxes; if revenue, then revenue; if respect,
then respect; if honor, then honor"* (Romans 13:7). It is much easier
to criticize this nation's leaders than to pray for them, but pray for
them is what believers must do. *"I urge, then, first of all, that
requests, prayers, intercession and thanksgiving be made for everyone—
for kings and all those in authority, that we may live peaceful and quiet
lives in all godliness and holiness"* (I Timothy 2:1-2).

Persecution in the United States

Throughout church history, Satan has attacked Christians. The
record begins in the Book of Acts. Satan used a political system—
the Roman Government—to persecute early believers. Does that
mean that Christians will be openly persecuted for their faith?

Outright persecution may happen at some point in the future,
but this has not been Satan's primary method of warfare against
Christians in the United States. Christians will increasingly be
rendered ineffective. But this will not come about as a result of gov-
ernment-sponsored violence. It will come about as a result of
spiritual deterioration.

Satan's primary means of attack for God's people in America
has been *deception*, not *persecution*. For centuries, Satan has worked
through governments to persecute Christians. He used the Roman
Government to crucify Christ, and he continued to use governments
to attack the apostles. During the Middle Ages, governments of
European nations allied themselves with organized religions to
persecute followers of Christ. In the Modern Era, Christians
trapped in communist lands have been starved, beaten, and tortured
for their faith. Satan has used repressive regimes to commit un-
speakable acts of evil against those who followed the cause of Christ.

But the founding of the American nation was a new event in
the spiritual history of the world. The United States, a new

nation, was established according to Christian principles. American law affirmed Christian beliefs, and early Americans established a tradition of liberty which promoted the free exercise of Christian activities. When this happened, Satan had to devise a different plan, and the plan he formulated would cause even greater damage to the church.

Rather than persecution, Satan initiated a campaign of lies and distortion. Satan would not overcome the Christian heritage through force and violence. He would not force believers to choose to follow Christ at the cost of personal pain and suffering. Rather, he would lull Christians to sleep; ensnare them in a web of doubt and denial. And when he worked his purpose, the people of the mighty nation would trade their Christian heritage for a contemptible counterfeit.

Refuse Credit Cards?

Should Christians avoid automated bank teller machines? Cut up their credit cards? Keep their savings at home in their mattresses?

As I have explained, the technology of the mark of the beast is already here, but not the effort for the government control of the economy John describes as the mark of the beast. It could well be that government control of the financial realm may be God's means of purging His people from the beast's economy. When that day comes, Christians will need to separate themselves from their dependence on the world and acknowledge more of their dependence on Him.

If the Christian community recognized the government effort to control financial relationships as the mark of the beast, there would likely be some opposition. Some Christians know from reading Revelation that they should not accept the beast's number. Perhaps Christians would refuse to accept the mark and still be able to receive an income and purchase the things they need, at least at first. But as the months pass, then a year or two, the government's thirst for power and the public's general mistrust and suspicion will emerge. Christians, and others who resist the mark, will come under greater pressure, and those who have lost their commitment to Jesus will accept the mark and yield to the beast-system.

As the economic conditions John refers to unfold in these last days, many will crave financial security. I would not attempt to offer financial advice. Everyone's financial condition is different, and I am not qualified to say exactly what you should or should not do with your finances. The Bible, does, however, provide guidance. As Christians, we should live within our means. It is easy, especially for young people today, to buy now, pay later and accumulate a large debt in order to possess all of the material things available. The seducing spirits of our world's system have implanted a deep desire for material acquisition. But the Christian life is not about giving in to selfish desires; it's about service and devotion to Jesus.

Examine the Lord's counsel to the church at Laodicea (Revelation 3:14-22). The Laodicean church typifies so much thinking in America today. They were a self-satisfied, self-righteous group who proclaimed, *"I am rich; I have acquired wealth and do not need a thing."* Jesus told them they were, in reality, *"wretched, pitiful, poor, blind and naked,"* and advised them to *"buy from me gold refined in the fire,"* to overcome their state of want. Jesus is not talking about the kind of gold stored at Fort Knox, of course. He's talking about becoming spiritually rich. And the only way to buy that kind of gold is through total commitment.

Many Christians are *involved* today, but it appears that few are *committed* to the teachings of Jesus; there is a vast difference between the two. It is easy to be involved because involvement amounts to human activity. We can be active in our local churches doing many works in the name of Jesus Christ, but that does not mean we are committed to Him. Remember the Pharisees? Their commitment was to a religion. Commitment to Jesus Christ is not something of the flesh, but of the Spirit. It must come from our inner beings. Deep commitment in our hearts means giving ourselves—our bodies, minds, personalities, natural talents, and abilities—to God so that He and His indwelling Spirit may use them to work His will. *"For it is God who works in you to will and to act according to his good purpose,"* (Philippians 2:13).

We are living in a period that requires all Christians to spend as much spare time and energy as possible seeking God — to be completely possessed by His Holy Spirit so that we may be guided through these deceptive times. The only thing that will carry us through in the days ahead is not our knowledge of all the various Bible doctrines, but what we know of the Lord Jesus Christ personally living in our hearts. What of the life of Christ has the Holy Spirit revealed in me and to me, and made a part of me? What we know of Christ spiritually, inwardly, — not our mental and intellectual knowledge of Him — will get us through. For me to live is Christ living in me (Galatians 2:20). Only He overcame the systems of the world (John 16:33).

CHAPTER 13

GOD'S NEXT MOVE IN AMERICA

During this period of history, God is allowing American Christians to be tested like never before through the beast-system, and the testing of our commitment to biblical standards is going to increase. Satan has used America's position in the world to develop in our people an attitude of self-sufficiency, independence, selfishness, and pride. This is how he has used the beast-system to attack the very fiber of our country's spiritual heritage and Christians' spiritual commitment and loyalty to our Lord Jesus Christ and His teachings. Our government's influence has been most deceitful, presented in the name of God while promoting the concept of a "great society" in which man attempts to control his own destiny. Satan is going to work through our systems to the limits God allows in his attempt to undermine and destroy our Christian heritage.

God's next move in dealing with the church in America will not be the rapture. There are those who teach that Christians will be taken out before the days of trouble begin. A message of, "Don't worry, Christians will be removed from the earth before tribulation comes," has appeal. But it is not the message I believe Scriptures teach. It is inconsistent with Scriptures. Jesus never promised that the Christian life would be free of trouble.

Christians who have survived Nazism and Communist torture have identified the pre-tribulation rapture teaching as a doctrine of escapism, as a uniquely American doctrine suitable only for those living in a land where profession of Christianity costs nothing. The message of these dear saints is that Jesus will sustain the faithful no matter what the trouble. God never abandons those who seek Him. This is the message that I believe the Scriptures teach.

The Lord's next move in our society, I believe, will be to prepare His bride. He will separate a body of believers to wage war against Satan. This remnant will be wholly committed to Christ.

Today it is easy to claim Christianity. One can say, "I am a Christian, too," when it is convenient, then live a self-centered life without consequence. But that will change. The time is coming when God will not trust His holy presence to those who are not wholly separated from the standards of the world. Those who attempt to mix with the world, who say they trust Jesus but cling to worldly ways and standards will face difficult times. Moral decay, economic ruin, and chaotic conditions of God's judgment from natural disasters are accelerating.

Christians Are to be At War with Satan

No one likes to think about going into heavy spiritual combat, especially when other aspects of life appear to be just fine. Peace and prosperity is the ear-tickling message so popular today. It is so much easier to go to church for entertainment rather than to prepare for spiritual battle. Warfare is exhaustive, stressful, expensive and dangerous.

Yet Christians must be warriors of the Lord. This is especially true here in America because our country has been the world's center of Christian teaching and activity during the last 300 years of the Church Age. The ways of Satan, as presented in Scripture, reveal that he has reserved his fiercest onslaughts for America in these last days. He systematically removes as many biblical standards as he can, then moves in to pillage and destroy. If we are going to prevent him from tearing down our families and our spiritual commitment along with them, we must fortify our means of resistance. It was never God's intention to draft a peacetime army. A peacetime army never wins any battles, because it never takes to the battlefield.

There is not a single Christian who has not been called to become a soldier in God's army. There is no option. You can only be one of three things: a warrior, a deserter, or a POW. Satan welcomes deserters and POW's because they support his cause by their inactivity. Inactive Christians give aid and comfort to the enemy.

We should be collecting our weapons for battle, not for a parade. Satan has declared war. We are in a war zone, one of the most heavily contested war zones the enemy has ever mustered against God's people, being carried out right here in our country through the beast-system as John prophesied.

It is past time for all born-again believers to take a stronger stand for God's standards. When we do not take this stand, we invite the world to question our love for God and our appreciation for the sacrifice Jesus made for our salvation. The lack of a clear stand also gives the world the freedom to challenge biblical standards. The testimony revealed through the lives of committed Christians demonstrating deep-seated attachment to biblical requirements is the only Christian message that will be heard *in this day when self-interest has replaced holy fear in so much teaching, and prosperity has replaced the cross in so much preaching.* It is time for us to show the world that it is our God, not the god of this world, who has the power. Our Commander-in-Chief is sovereign, not the world's leader.

The world so desperately needs to see an army of dedicated Christians. We must begin to apply the soothing power of the spiritual ointment God has given us to heal society from the hurt and pain inflicted by the enemy. Let us prove the power of God in our lives by declaring war against sin and start a revolution for seeking righteousness. We must show the world, by the fruits of our lives, that we follow a more powerful God than they do.

For me and my family, learning that the beast of Revelation 13 is the United States Government has motivated us to increase our commitment. We have learned of the need to be constantly alert to our spiritual commitment to Jesus, to the spiritual battles in this world. God warned us of things that have caused many others great pain.

Learning the identity of the beast has caused us to see that something is terribly wrong in this society. Not too long ago, a majority of Americans acknowledged moral standards. Even those who did not participate actively in churches respected God and the testimony of those who followed Him. But this fear of the Lord has evaporated during the past few years. The present generation demonstrates their inability to draw the line between good and bad, meaningful and ritualistic, beautiful and ugly, sacred and profane. Christians and non-Christians alike have abandoned the holy fear of the Lord that brings discernment of right and wrong.

Those who seek the Lord's protection during the days ahead must search their own hearts. Before anything else can happen, I believe the Christian must repent of apathy. Only then can the Lord prepare us for battle. Commitment must follow. Not commitment to a church organization. Church membership, attendance, and church-sponsored activities can help empower believers. But this should not be confused with true commitment. A heart of obedience to God's Word and a holy fear of the Lord causes a person to cling to what is right for fear of doing anything else. Surviving the troubled days ahead begins and ends with being completely, utterly dependent on Jesus.

My wife, Barbara, and I have learned much about living the Christian life since our research of the Scriptures confirmed that the United States Government has become the beast-superpower of Revelation 13. We sincerely pray that, during these last days, what we have learned and presented in my books will add nourishment to your spiritual diet.

Additional copies of this study book on the beast are available from the address below.

Christian Life Outreach
6438 E. Jenan Drive
Scottsdale, AZ 85254
Call (602)-998-4136 or use order form on back page.

Other than the necessary funds to cover expenses, donations for my books are used to help the poor and needy through Help The World/Direct. This is a unique Christian ministry in which 100 percent of all donations go directly to help those who are suffering. I have never taken money for anything I have written.

About the Author

Books and newsletters by the author have been written solely for the purpose of sharing the message God has given him.

Work

Bob Fraley is a corporate executive with a subsidiary of Alcoa.

Family

He lives with his wife, Barbara, in Scottsdale, Arizona. They have raised nine children: three boys of their own and six guardian children that joined the family in 1969 after a tragic auto accident took their parents. Today, all nine serve the Lord.

Christian Education

Soon after moving to Arizona in 1973, he was instrumental in founding Paradise Valley Christian School. It became one of the major Christian schools in metropolitan Phoenix, serving families from more than 50 churches. He served as President of the school for 17 years; and continues to serve on the board of Phoenix Christian High School.

Church

He has served as an elder, board member, and adult Bible study teacher at Trinity Church, Assembly of God.

Founder
Christian Life Outreach
Help the World/Direct

He recently founded Help the World/Direct, an outreach of Christian Life Outreach, a nonprofit corporation he organized to aid the poor and needy and teach and distribute Christian materials. Help the World/Direct is a unique Christian ministry in that 100 percent of the donations go directly to help those who are suffering. All of the overhead expenses associated with operating the organization are made up of volunteer labor and the author's personal funds.

References

Spiritual, professional, and corporation leaders from around the country have written letters about his character and testimony that are available on request.

Personal Note From the Author

Like many others in America, Barbara and I love our country and the freedoms with which we have been blessed. This Bible study of Revelation 13 comes in the hope that it will help others become better prepared for the spiritual challenges in these times.

FOOTNOTES

Chapter One
1. Zondervan Publishing House, *Greek-English New Testament* (Grand Rapids, MI 1975) p. 751.
2. Thomas Sowell, *Ethnic America*, Basic Books 1981.

Chapter Three
1. Admiral Robert A. Theobald, *The Final Secret of Pearl Harbor*, serialized in *U.S. News and World Report*, April 2, 1954, p. 51.

Chapter Eleven
1. *Los Angeles Times*, 25 August 1974.
2. *Wall Street Journal*, 11 November 1981.

BOOK ORDER FORM

*Other important biblical principles about living
the Christian life in America during these last days
are shared in...*

QUANTITY	BOB FRALEY's books	EACH	TOTAL AMOUNT
	THE BEAST OF REVELATION 13	$ 7.95	
	THE LAST DAYS IN AMERICA	7.95	
	HOLY FEAR	7.95	
	Total Order Handling & Postage		2.00
ORDERED BY:		TOTAL	$

Name

_____

Address

_____

_____

Phone Orders call **1-602-998-4136**

Mail Order Form with check or money order to:

Christian Life Outreach
6438 E. Jenan Drive
Scottsdale, AZ 85254

Please Note: *All net proceeds from the sale of these
books are used to help the poor and needy.
You will receive a Tax deductible receipt for
that amount allowed by law.*